Building
AUTHENTIC CONFIDENCE
In Children

Dr. Spencer Taintor
with RaeAnne Marie Scargall

Building Authentic Confidence In Children

Acclaim for
Building Authentic Confidence in Children

"Authentic confidence is a concept that has a special place in today's society. It is particularly relevant because of the challenges we have wrought with raising a generation of 'trophy kids'. Although there are any number of exceptions, many of the Millennials demonstrate the characteristics of entitled adults who struggle with life's challenges and show little to no resilience. For the last 20 years, higher education has been forced to respond to an increasing number of students entering its institutions academically underprepared. That challenge has been exacerbated by these same students fleeing at the first sign of failure...a case of social promotion running headlong into institutional inflexibility. Spence Taintor addresses these and more issues and what educators and parents can do to change the paradigm. This book is a must read for educators and parents and anyone who has ever wondered how we can 'change the game' with our Millennial Generation."

-Dr. Harry Muir
Special Assistant to the Chancellor for Southeast Wisconsin Initiatives; University of Wisconsin

"Kids need to be good with taking chances to build their confidence. We all learn that failures can teach us more than wins!"

-Colin Drummond
Ogilvy & Mather

"Authentic confidence is the perfect blend of two important distinctions that are critical for leaders to be successful in our fast paced and ever changing world. The 'authentic' component is the courage to be yourself, passionately pursue the things you believe in, and respect the unique cultures of those around you. The 'confidence' component also contains a deep connection to courage, as it's truly needed to eradicate the negative mental chatter that constantly rattles in your head and says you can't do it. It's the critical learning from failure that plays such an important role in being both authentic and confident, especially when learning from failure is your friend, not the end! Dr. Taintor's perspective on the confidence deficiency of our children and building confidence inside and outside of the classroom are spot-on in offering new insights that can accelerate a really positive, long term leadership impact in the way our youth can think and act."

-Bob Cancalosi
Director of Global Leadership Programs, GE Crotonville

Quantity order requests can be emailed to:
publishing@rejilaberje.com
Or mailed to:
Reji Laberje Writing And Publishing
Publishing Orders
234 W. Broadway Street
Waukesha, WI 53186

ISBN-10: 0692736913
ISBN-13: 978-0692736913

BISAC Codes:
EDU034000 EDUCATION / Educational Policy & Reform / General
EDU003000 EDUCATION / Aims & Objectives
EDU029000 EDUCATION / Teaching Methods & Materials / General

Writing and Publishing

www.rejilaberje.com

Dr. Spencer Taintor

For my wife, Elizabeth, who has been instrumental in helping me build my own authentic confidence.

For my children, Spencer and Emma, who make me smile and laugh every day.

TABLE OF CONTENTS

FOREWORD

Building Authentic Confidence in Children is a Reji Laberje Writing and Publishing interactive text. Scan the QR code below to learn more about Dr. Spencer Taintor and his message.

Find a free QR scanner for your smart device via a search through your device's app store. Then, you can scan the QR code with your smart device to open Dr. Taintor's website.

Find more information at:

www.spencertaintor.com

Try it out now by scanning the QR code:

Building
AUTHENTIC CONFIDENCE
In Children

Building Authentic Confidence In Children

CHAPTER ONE

INTRODUCTION

Matt paused and looked at me blank-faced—but there was this twinkle in his eye.

"I got it," he announced.

A big smile enthusiastically appeared on his face, and I could immediately sense his confidence propelling him forward.

At this time several years ago, I was teaching regular and advanced high school chemistry in Miami, Florida. I'd been teaching the unit of measurement called the mole. If you are like most, the concept of the mole is probably still illusive, and might even conjure, "Not that again!" Some may remember that a mole describes a substance's number of atoms, molecules, etc.

This student, Matt, had come to me after school several days this particular week. Our chemistry lab was similar to most schools', with glassware on the counters and lab benches and stools spread throughout the room. It was different from the science class spaces of today, with both a traditional teaching space and lab area within the same room. Matt was struggling with the mole unit of measurement. He was trying to comprehend in his mind, in any way possible, a mole of something. Matt was highly intelligent and could easily solve a calculus problem faster than many other students.

And in that moment, Matt finally understood it, at the level needed to move forward in chemical computations. It was amazing to witness his struggles—and even failures—with trying to understand this concept, and then the rush of self-esteem he gained in his "ah-ha!" moment. Afterward, Matt was unstoppable in chemistry. He finished the course with a B-. One may wonder why that would be considered an achievement...a B- is just average to many. Matt's achievement was that he developed the confidence to tackle a subject, over and over again, even if it sometimes meant failure. He worked through his own barriers and achieved something of his own accord.

For Matt, failure became an acceptable option because it was now part of the learning process he'd experienced firsthand—he achieved comfort with not always succeeding. Through these classroom experiences, he developed the confidence to take on new things, regardless of the outcome; no matter the final product, he recognized and appreciated the process of learning.

Many students fail to develop the confidence required to put themselves out there or chase a dream. They have a fear of failure, even though it's an essential part of the learning process. Once students recognize this, they can develop healthy and productive confidence that becomes a catalyst for great opportunities.

As a child, I struggled with phonics and grammar. I've come to realize that I showed a specific weakness in phonological development, and maybe even some signs of Dyslexia. My parents thought I was just lazy because my IQ tested higher than normal.

When I was a second grader at a public school in Dade County, FL, in the mid-1970s, my teacher was a tough traditional disciplinarian. She once picked a student up out of his chair by his ear and marched him, ear still in hand, all the way to the principal's office. One particular day, I was writing comments about a book we'd read—*The Adventures of Tom Sawyer*. As the disciplinarian looked over my shoulder, she chastised me in front of the class for my grammar and writing style. She said, "Why are you saying it that way?" and, "This does not make sense—that's stupid." It was humiliating, to say the least, and it also destroyed my confidence in writing and grammar altogether as these comments occurred continuously in that classroom. What purpose did making these comments serve? I was at a critical point in my development and needed to be engaged in the process and understanding of learning, yet I had little support from my teacher.

For several years my parents had me work with a tutor on phonics, grammar, and writing. Believe it or not, it wasn't until writing my Ph.D. Program dissertation at age 33 that I truly gained any confidence in my writing abilities.

Similarly, when I was in fifth grade, my teacher presented our class with a national science invention competition. It was optional and not all students in my class participated. At that age, I would spend hours with Legos building cities, planes—whatever my imagination could conjure. Creativity has never been an obstacle for me. Despite my writing struggles, I could certainly speak at an elevated level, due to my parents involving me and my siblings in adult conversations at home and at social functions. My dad was a graduate of Emory, and while my mom did not go to college, they both encouraged us to read and stay current with the local and national news. Education was always a priority for my parents.

In preparation for the contest, I spent hours at home thinking about what I could invent that would help people. I called on my personal struggles with putting words on paper, as I believed that I was not alone in my difficulties with written communication. I came up with an idea for a computer or computer chip that transcribed spoken words onto paper. It was like an embryonic version of today's Dragon Dictation program. It was "forward thinking" in a time when pong had just come out and computer programming was in its infancy in schools.

I was so proud to present my invention. I remember two of my classmates telling me that such an invention was ridiculous. Additionally, I received a letter back from the organization stating that such an invention was impossible, and therefore, my submission would not move forward in the competition. My confidence was shot yet again in yet another area of my psyche. What purpose did this serve? Why wouldn't they instead challenge students to research and demonstrate that something seemingly impossible might, in fact, be possible? That learning experience itself would've been far richer than the outcome, but apparently it was easier to just shoot down the idea than help me grow as a student.

Not unlike many children, I spent the better part of my formative years seeking approval as I tried to build my confidence. I questioned my ability. It drove me to work hard, not for the sake of learning, but merely for validation while I struggled with gaining the external feedback needed to bolster my internal strength and self-perception. I realized that without confidence, I was held back—not by teachers, but by my own experiences. Even though they were not to blame, teachers still could have provided the support I needed to turn my frustrating failures from disappointment and discouragement into learning and skill development.

These experiences taught me throughout my business, entrepreneurship, teaching, administrative careers, and life, that fostering confidence in students is an essential key in building them a substantial foundation for entering the world. As we continue to refine and improve educational processes for students, it would be remiss to not encourage and challenge them to ignite ideas and learn from failures, rather than destructively criticize and dismiss them to get through content for content's sake. Whether the classroom is in a private or inner-city public school, the world of business or nonprofit, teaching individuals to develop inner-confidence is essential in preparing them for life.

In recent years, reports from the Child Trends DataBank show an increase in hopelessness in students. While psychological research shows that there is a normal drop in self-esteem in middle school, these reports' numbers are drastically higher than normal. This is cause for alarm.

It is imperative that students develop adequate confidence and self-esteem for tackling life challenges and obstacles. Why would we want students to enter the workforce feeling hopeless and with a lack of confidence? In a time and age when the United States and many other developed and developing nations are seeking ways to be leaders in innovation, educators need to pause and understand that promoting confidence in our adolescents is a much-needed attribute for their success. Educators also need to understand that while content is necessary, we have the responsibility to teach the skills that help turn all experiences, whether good or bad, into learning moments. We need to build their confidence in a way that allows them to learn from failures, rather than be discouraged and disenfranchised.

Throughout many conversations I've had with VPs and CEOs in various industries, I've noticed a trend. There is a growing need for our future workforce to be flexible, adaptable, calculated in taking risks, lifelong learners, and individuals not afraid of failure. The world of tomorrow is speeding up, and the incoming workforce's ability to tackle new challenges, reinvent themselves and their careers, and be self-reliant will lead to success and realistic visions for their futures. In order to exhibit these traits and interact in this future environment, we need individuals to be confident—not over-confident or under-confident, but confident enough to extend themselves in uncomfortable environments and know that if they fail, they will learn from it and move on. Young people need to develop confidence so they can tackle a project or assignment without being spoon-fed directions to achieve the end goal. Most young adults are afraid to make mistakes and hold an underlying belief that if they are not "perfect," they will not succeed, which leads them to be withdrawn and risk-averse.

We need students to be more independent doers and thinkers. Author Gever Tulley (2011) suggests, "If you're over thirty, you probably walked to school, played on the monkey bars, and learned to high-dive at the public pool. If you're younger, it's unlikely you did any of these things. Yet, has the world become that much more dangerous? Statistically, no, but our society has created pervasive fears about letting kids be independent—and the consequences for our kids are serious" (p. 1). Our society continues to try and protect our kids at all costs so they do not fail; they request that teachers stop using red ink when grading papers and even cease from giving meaningful feedback during class time. It's seen as negative, even though the intent is to provide a blanket of protection. We are failing miserably at preparing students for a world that will not be risk-free.

According to a study by University College London, risk-taking behavior peaks during adolescence. In order to grow adolescents' confidence, we must first allow these experiences of age-related risks to take place, while simultaneously helping them learn why they failed or succeeded. By testing these boundaries, adolescents will develop life skills and find their identities during these years. This is when they learn, via experience, to develop confidence. Our failure to let them take risks may explain why so many young adults (between the ages of 22 and 35) still live at home, haven't started their careers, or have never experienced a serious relationship. Developing confidence at an early age by facing and overcoming risks would have prepared them for life's challenges, such as moving away from home, launching a career, or getting married.

We need our students entering the workforce as self-starters. We need to ensure that the next generations have the toolboxes of skills necessary to solve problems in an elastic and fluctuating way—not just by depending on a set of directions.

Roald Amundsen was the first person to reach the South Pole. His philosophy was that, through the process of successes and failures, one discovers the strength and endurance needed to prepare for the unexpected storm. He succeeded in reaching the South Pole because he built his confidence over time. As he led his team on the expedition, they certainly encountered times where success seemed unattainable, but Amundsen had the confidence to find solutions and push forward. Jim Collins states that confidence comes not from motivational speeches, blind hope, or unfounded optimism, but from actual achievement attained through trial and error and consistently working hard toward goals, no matter the conditions. It is through these personal experiences that individuals develop their inner strengths and responsibilities and build themselves toolboxes for shaping their life-goal achievements. However, these experiences do not begin *after* a formal education—they are like a foundation for a house. If a foundation's base is cracked, the house can crumble. If we do not build the confidence of our students in a meaningful and realistic way early on, they will not have the foundations to build their careers upon.

What leads a person to become a CEO of an organization? What leads a person to say, "I can do this, even though I have not in the past"? My own experiences have taught me that when I was an entrepreneur, I took on assignments and challenges that built my confidence. I often failed, but my learning from those failures was pivotal—though I was not taught this in my formative educational years. As I developed confidence, it became clear that I could push myself, and I would find a way to lead, grow, and inspire those around me. So, how do we build confidence in our children?

Research about adolescent self-esteem and confidence is extensive and provides a framework for us to determine how to build confidence. We know that self-esteem is an internal emotional trait, while confidence is developed through external experiences. Decades of research has been conducted on child self-esteem. However, the practical research that investigates applicable classroom methods is not as extensive and provides few hands-on tools for teachers to implement this research. There is a clear need for this as we investigate the research of building confidence in children, and the effects of a lack of confidence within today's workforce. As we continue to connect research with application in the next chapters, there are clear paths by which both a child's classroom and outside environments grow confidence. This growth is necessary for interacting and thriving in the world.

Building authentic, genuine, balanced confidence is the essential key that provides both the safety nets parents and educators want for children, and the tools they need to face challenges both today and tomorrow. Authentic confidence is not developed in a risk-free environment, but through encouragement and support in facing challenges. Confidence is the key to a new generation of adults who inspire innovation and lead a world in need of direction. Building genuine confidence in our children will not be easy for teachers or parents, but it is essential for creating capable leaders for tomorrow. How we achieve this will develop over time and become clearer through our own successes and failures.

We cannot sit back and expect our current approaches to children's confidence development to be sufficient. Let's start the conversation: how to build authentic confidence today for the leaders of tomorrow.

PART ONE

THE CONFIDENCE DEFICIENCY

CHAPTER TWO

CHILDREN'S SELF-ESTEEM

*"The greatest mistake in life is to be continually
fearing that you will make one."*
—*Elbert Hubbard*

Since the early 1870s and well before that, psychologists have tried to understand adolescents: their behaviors, growth stages, and every aspect of childhood development. As an educator, I recognize the need to understand and research how and what make children "tick." Hundreds of volumes have been written about the adolescent years and the logical learning patterns children phase through.

The interesting thing about adolescent psychology is that it's always changing because our world is always changing. I certainly believe that a child's growth has to do with both nature and nurture. A child cannot change the genetic pool he came from; however, the environment he interacts in and is exposed to can swing the pendulum from one side to the other. I have seen this happen, especially with children growing up in poverty. Honestly, how can children focus on learning and developing healthy self-esteem (or healthy lives, for that matter) if they're unsure they'll eat that day? When you take capable children out of poverty and surround them with resources and support, they thrive. As we dive into the research behind building confidence, we must keep environmental factors in perspective, as they are constantly changing—from technological and communication innovations to shifting global issues that impact larger groups of people. Children are not immune to these factors, no matter how small or large.

My own daughter knows how to e-mail, Skype, and navigate a computer at age seven. In addition, she is aware of global conflict and even climate change. This is not because our family is extremely technological or we make our children watch the news every night. It is because children hear conversations, see newspapers in stores, read headlines, and even discuss things at school through service projects and literature. This being the case, how could we not recognize, as a society and in our research, that our adolescents' environments are in a constant state of change, and that the research will need to be continually updated and adapted?

That said, there is widely supported research in the areas of child self-esteem. It's been known for more than 150 years that a child's emotional development strongly influences his or her relationships with others, behavior, and learning. Current research emphasizes the adolescent years as a critically important period for the development of future mental health and self-esteem. Children with a healthy sense of self-esteem feel confident in achieving tasks, their relationships with adults, and dealing with obstacles. Low self-esteem has been shown to often lead to learning disabilities, disciplinary problems, and depression. The research presented in this chapter highlights findings related to self-esteem and confidence in children.

As we begin to look at the research associated with children's self-esteem and confidence, it is important to recognize there is a difference between the two—but a relationship does exist in which it is hard to have one without the other (Stankov and Kleitman, 2008). A simple way to understand the difference is to consider self-esteem an internal experience and confidence an external experience. Self-esteem is described as the way we feel about ourselves; it's a reflection of our inner sense of self-value and entitlement (Kleitman, 2008). On the other hand, confidence is a reflection of the way we experience ourselves in our environment. Confidence in children can be described simply as the way they feel about interacting and engaging with friends, teachers, subject material, and other things in the world. Confidence acts as a skill and can be learned through trial and error. Self-esteem in children can be seen as a reflection of their inner-sense of self-value; they feel they serve a role within the family, classroom, and society. Self-esteem, if low, can cause much greater difficulty for children as they grow. If children lack confidence in an area but their self-esteem is healthy, that self-esteem will be a buffer and solid foundation for facing and learning from experiences. Children with healthy self-esteem have shown to be more resilient and willing to try something, and regardless of the outcome, still feel good about themselves (Kleitman, 2008). Children with very low self-esteem are almost always ultra-critical of themselves (Kleitman, 2008). They are usually overly hard on themselves, even when they achieve something quite significant—they never reward themselves. They will shy away from compliments and do not receive them well. They tend to value themselves and their thoughts, actions, and successes less than others'.

It is one's personal self-evaluation that leads to high or low self-esteem (Baumeister, Campbell, Krueger, and Vohs, 2003). High self-esteem manifests in children with a positive evaluation of self. Low self-esteem refers to a negative view of the self. Baumeister, Campbell, Krueger, and Vohs (2003) summarize that high self-esteem may "refer to an accurate, justified, balanced appreciation of one's worth as a person and one's successes and competencies, but it can also refer to an inflated, arrogant, grandiose, unwarranted sense of conceited superiority over others. By the same token, low self-esteem can be either an accurate, well-founded understanding of one's shortcomings as a person or a distorted, even pathological sense of insecurity and inferiority" (p. 2).

Nathaniel Branden, a leading figure in the self-esteem movement, stated that self-esteem has "profound consequences for every aspect of our existence" (Branden, 1994, p. 5), and that he "cannot think of a single psychological problem—from anxiety and depression, to fear of intimacy or of success, to spouse battery or child molestation, that is not traceable to the problem of low self-esteem" (Branden, 1984, p. 12).

While self-esteem is a critical component of a child's development, the research on it is evolving as the world is evolving. There are many theories on how low or high self-esteem affect both high- and low-income children with either involved or absent parents. However, it is clear from research that there is no evidence of developed societies suffering from rampant low self-esteem. Self-esteem seems generally high in most North American research data. Regardless of race, gender, or socioeconomic status, Americans appear to live in a "culture of self-worth" (Twenge & Campbell, 2001, p. 325).

Research from Germany and Norway has also shown positive effects regarding the self-esteem, behavioral stability, and cognitive development of children who participated in groups that performed challenging tasks (Rönnau-Böse & Fröhlich-Gildhoff, 2009). Many countries have long-known that a child's self-esteem plays an important role in his or her growth. In a Rönnau-Böse, M., and Fröhlich-Gildhoff (2009) study, the concept of resilience and the person-centered view were compatible with each other, resulting in more positive, stronger self-esteem, and thus greater academic achievement.

As we examine this phenomenon through research, it is already easy to see the effects every day around us. Our society has moved from the "look at us" to the "look at me" perspective, which is obviously prevalent in today's media, corporations, and Western society in general. Bushman and Baumeister (1998) have even suggested through their findings that the rate of narcissism, a result of too much self-esteem, has been on the rise in America for some time. Narcissism can be described as a highly favorable, even grandiose view of self, sense of uniqueness, illusion of personal brilliance, and belief that one is entitled to privileges above others (Baumeister, Campbell, Krueger, and Vohs, 2003). This type of overinflated self-esteem has profound effects in later life and is rooted in actions, policies, and parenting styles that actively seek to avoid low self-esteem in children. As a nation, we have swung the pendulum too far to one side, and we are now seeing some of these negative effects. Jean Twenge (2009) describes this best when he talks about the "everybody gets a trophy" mentality, which implies that one will be rewarded just for showing up. That won't build true self-esteem or confidence; instead, it builds a false sense of accomplishment. Such behaviors by parents, teachers, coaches, and society have led to oversized self-esteem in our children, which manifests itself in narcissistic behaviors in adulthood. It is the development of a healthy, *balanced* sense of self-esteem that leads children to approach life and its challenges with a "can-do" attitude.

How do we know this? Bowles (1999) measured the self-esteem of a group of students after they completed a semester and had received their grades. He found that an adolescent's view of his or her self-esteem is a result, not a cause, of doing well in school. This will be important to remember later as we examine ways teachers can raise confidence and self-esteem in students in authentic ways.

Skaalvik and Hagtvet (1990) measured students' self-concepts of their academic abilities. They concluded that self-concept of ability connects the dots between academic performance and self-esteem. Specifically, doing well in school leads to considering oneself good at academics, which in turn can boost self-esteem. They also discovered data, however loosely correlated, that suggests that thinking highly of oneself can lead to better schoolwork. However, practitioners must be careful not to take such research and assume that copious praise of academic performance will lead to greater self-esteem or a more genuine ability to master skills and content. It is a balance that must be carefully navigated.

Baumeister, Campbell, Krueger, and Vohs (2003) summarize this by saying that "high self-esteem has value in causing people to persist longer in the face of failure" (p. 6). Persistence allows for self-confidence development due to the likelihood of more options and chances to achieve favorable results. While the risk of pushing self-esteem into a narcissistic realm is certainly a concern, creating an environment in which students can grow self-esteem in an authentic and genuine manner will lead to higher academic performance and greater future growth. Without self-esteem, confidence must fight an uphill battle to properly develop. Self-esteem must exist in order for an adolescent to persist or even attempt a challenge where failure is a possibility. It is through these challenges that not only is confidence built, but self-esteem is cemented, and this encourages further exploration and experimentation.

Buhrmester, et al. (1988) offer research showing that students with positive self-esteem have tendencies to initiate interpersonal contacts and relationships. In groups (school, business, social, etc.), individuals with positive self-esteem are more willing to speak up and propose action than those with low self-esteem. This may allow them to lead and take initiatives, thus giving them more exposure and more confidence with how they approach different circumstances.

As previously stated, an adolescent's ability to develop a healthy sense of confidence is reliant upon a foundation of positive self-esteem—one cannot exist without the other. We cannot expect a child with low self-esteem to have the confidence to attempt something with the probability of failure. On the other hand, however, we cannot expect a child with excessive self-esteem to develop the confidence to attempt the same things, due to the same fear of failure. Extremely low and excessive amounts of self-esteem both result in a fear of failure, and therefore a lack of confidence.

So what role does confidence play in a child's life? If self-esteem is the inner-thoughts and value systems of adolescents and adults, how do we develop confidence before we reach adulthood? Are there certain experiential attributes that help build or break down that confidence?

It is critical to understand that the environment in which experiences occur determines a great deal about the outcome of building confidence. When considering environment, we should note these observations of both confident and non-confident children by Määttä and Järvelä (2013).

> Children recognize themselves as capable of facing difficult or challenging tasks (Zimmerman and Kitsantas, 2005), expend more effort and persistence (Milton, Brown, and Lent, 1991), display adaptive and mastery behaviors by self-regulating their learning processes (Zimmerman, 2002; Bandura, 1997; Seifert, 2004) and experience few

adverse emotional reactions when they encounter difficulties (Bandura, 1997). Learners who are not confident or perceive themselves as incapable may avoid tasks that they perceive to be challenging (Zimmerman, 2002; Bandura, 1997) and are likely to behave in a performance-oriented manner (Dweck, 1986) (p. 315).

This clearly indicates that the classroom experiences a child may have can likely provide a foundation for achievement and motivation for academic success. There are other contributing factors, as well, and these are the foundation of Bandura's (1986) concept of reciprocal determinism. Bandura viewed that (a) personal factors in the form of cognition, affect, and biological events, (b) behavior, and (c) environmental influences create interactions resulting in a triadic reciprocity. This model illustrates the different factors that come into play when children are developing confidence.

Model of Reciprocal Determinism

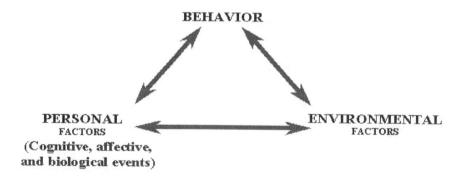

Ensuring that these three factors are positively maximized will aid in confidence growth. This does not mean children have to be in well-behaved classrooms with the best facilities and strong support from home in order to attain confidence. I believe that children can build confidence by having teachers who create this three-factor environment within their classrooms. For example, in many classrooms, children do not receive enough constructive feedback about their work or learning skills, nor are they taught strategies for evaluating their own performances and learning (Whitebread, 2012; Perry, Phillips, and Hutchinson, 2006). This missing piece disrupts the three-point model through either the personal cognitive factors or through the supportive classroom environment. Without formative feedback to provide guidance on how to improve or overcome a learning roadblock, children will fail to develop the confidence to accomplish the task or succeed in different learning environments. Children in these instances have struggled to build the accurate knowledge and skills required to effectively manage their learning (Winne and Perry, 2000; Zimmerman and Bandura, 1994). Bandura (1997) believes that teachers interpret their pupils' successes and failures through their own personal perspectives, forgetting that children themselves might attribute their successes or failures to entirely different factors.

It has been the focus of some research to try and identify how children evaluate their own learning. The challenge is to engage youngsters in discussions about their experiences in different classroom situations in order to focus on skills that progress their confidence levels. The goal for teachers is to allow students to self-regulate their learning. Teachers must help build strategies to guide and enhance students' learning processes (Zimmerman and Schunk, 2008). Research has focused on confidence as a means to explore learners' beliefs about their abilities to perform effectively and to succeed in specific situations (Bandura, 1997; Zimmerman and Kitsantas, 2005).

However, confidence is not a skill in itself. One cannot teach confidence—it must be built. Confidence is what a learner can do with his or her acquired skills under certain conditions, and the aptitude to coordinate skills in changing and challenging situations (Maddux, 2002). Therefore, confidence is built by developing coping skills through successes and failures with academic and non-academic goals. Confidence is built with the learner's belief in his or her capability to learn from an experience, rather than acceptance of whatever outcome is had. The strength of this belief is derived from various sources in different learning situations (Bandura, 1997).

Four different types of experiences help to establish a strong learner's confidence: mastery experience, vicarious experience, verbal and social persuasions, and emotional and physiological states (Bandura, 1994). Research seems to conclude that the most effective way to create a strong sense of confidence is through mastery experiences (Bandura, 1997). As children complete a goal or assignment, they interpret and evaluate the results (Palmer, 2006). These interpretations develop a student's belief in his or her competence and enhance confidence in accomplishing similar or related tasks under different contexts and conditions (Usher, 2008). When students understand why they succeeded or failed in a task or goal, they develop confidence in the ability to tackle similar challenges in the future. However, it is important to note that if substantial failures occur before a sense of confidence is firmly established, learners may falter in their ability to tackle tasks or goals (Van Dinther, Dochy, and Segers, 2011; Bandura, 1997). This is why it is imperative for teachers to be a supportive foundation for learners throughout failures and help them realize what went wrong and how they can work to overcome it. In turn, this will help build confidence in overcoming other kinds of setbacks or roadblocks in learning and life.

Adolescents with confidence can view a state of tension as motivating, whereas those with low confidence tend to interpret tension or stress as weakness (Van Dinther, Dochy, and Segers, 2011). The environment around them plays a role in supporting and testing confidence. This is a tricky balance for teachers to navigate in their classrooms, alongside handling the consequences of negative experiences that deteriorate students' confidence.

The confidence levels children witness in others affect their own confidence, as well. Seeing peers succeed by sustained efforts raises learners' beliefs that they, too, can master comparable activities required to succeed (George, Feltz, and Chase, 1992). On the other hand, observing classmates fail, despite great effort, may also lower learners' opinions of their own confidence and undermine their efforts (Schunk and Meece, 2006). Teachers need to be aware of the entire classroom environment and monitor the transparency of students' failures and how they are perceived by their classmates.

I recently witnessed this firsthand at a morning assembly where a fifth grader was to recite a poem in front of 200 parents and students from multiple grade levels. Other students in her grade had recited poems on prior days, but for this student, this task was certainly a struggle. As she began to recite the poem, she broke down after the first word and began to cry. She indicated she could not go on. She was given the option to take a few minutes to collect herself and try again, or wait for another day. As the assembly was coming to an end, she was asked if she wanted to try again. We watched her muster all her strength to walk up and recite. As she began, we could see her concentration and will. When she finished her poem, the crowd erupted in applause. It was definitely a mountain climbed. What happened afterward was the truly amazing part, though. Students from all grades were commenting on how courageous she was and how proud of her they were. You could see how her internal struggle and victory in that moment encouraged and inspired those around her, and maybe even elevated other students' confidence in overcoming similar obstacles.

When children are building their confidence through their own self-appraisal skills, they tend to depend on trusted others to provide evaluative feedback about their performances (Bandura, 1994). These could be peers as well as teachers. Määttä and Järvelä (2013) identified three types of interactive contexts, namely child-teacher-task, child-task, and child-child-task. The child-teacher-task context was the most typical one observed in supporting adolescents' confidence. It must be noted that this context is directly tied to environment—the environment is key. In multiple studies, children who experienced low confidence did not receive support and feedback from a teacher. A teacher's evaluation of students (both verbally and nonverbally) is significant because students know the teacher is the most familiar with their academic capabilities (Pajares, 2006). Overall, the findings from E. Määttä and S. Järvelä (2013) provide guidelines for how teachers can "scaffold the confidence of young learners by involving them in greater insight into the factors, classroom structures, and practices that children believe can undermine their success" (p. 321). It is imperative that children reflect on their performances, both good and bad. It is through this reflection, with the help of their teachers, that their academic skills and self-regulatory practices will improve (Grau and Whitebread, 2012). As we know from prior research, this interaction between teacher and student creates a positive outcome and mastery of dealing both psychologically and emotionally with success and failure. This mastery then leads to confidence growth and becomes a future tool for when a similar situation presents itself.

Dr. Carol Dweck of Standford University offers research that clearly supports the environment as a determining factor in students' confidence. Specifically, she has looked at the praise of students and how that relates to academic confidence. Her research analyzed a fifth-grade population in New York City. She gave each child in the research pool an IQ test, and then provided a single phrase of praise. The two different praises were, "You must be smart at this," or, "You must have worked really hard." The students were then given a choice of two tests. The first was a collection of puzzles that were described by the research assistants as difficult—but worth a try because the student would learn a lot from it. The other test was described as easy. Over 90% of the students originally praised for their efforts chose the harder test. The children praised for their intelligence mostly chose the easy test. In subsequent tests, Dweck found that students who were praised for their efforts compared to those who were praised for being smart scored 30% higher. She explained that focusing on effort gives children an element of their experience that they can have control over, and therefore be in the driver's seat for their successes (Dweck, 1986).

When looking at Dweck's research combined with previous data, it becomes clear that authentic confidence is not grown in students by telling them they are smart. Authentic confidence is achieved by getting them to work hard and garner feedback on how to improve. Please do not get me wrong—praise is not all bad. There is a time and place for praise, but if we are to raise children with healthy and authentic confidence, we must develop in them the tools needed to face challenges. Children who grow up with too much praise may avoid risk later in life and even develop narcissistic behaviors. They will also lack the persistence necessary for working through challenges.

False praise can come in the forms of, "You are so smart," or, "You worked your hardest." Telling children that they worked hard on something when they did not is just as bad as saying they are smart for the sake of praise, thinking that saying such will magically make them "better." Being realistic about the situation in a supportive way will help children develop a reliable toolbox, push them to strive for more, and exceed expectations.

The negative effects of false praise are more evident than ever by the current number of college freshmen dropouts. The United States has seen a steady increase in the number of freshmen who do not return to class. Some studies place the national trend at upward of 60% of freshmen. This trend has become even more prevalent as the Millennial Generation has entered college. This is the generation of "everyone gets a trophy" that was not parented with negative or even critical feedback. This group has been more susceptible to the inflation of self-esteem and confidence, to the point where they do not want to take risks or face challenges unless success is absolutely assured. Lowery (2004) indicated that Millennial students often have overinflated confidence in their academic skills that can make them unaware of their true academic capabilities. This can lead to struggle and eventual dropout, all due to a lack of genuine, authentic confidence. If their confidence is developed in a way that supports them, they can find new solutions, skills, and tools with which to persevere and find a successful pathway in a possible storm of failure. I believe this data alone is enough to show K-12 educators what skills are most important for adolescents to grow and excel in life.

The research presented in this chapter provides clear groundwork showing that self-esteem in children is critical to the development of confidence. As previously stated, one cannot thrive without the other. However, confidence that is built in an authentic and realistic way provides a pathway for students to succeed in spite of failure. Teachers and parents need to provide a realistic assessment of a child's performance, while simultaneously guiding him or her through the attainment of skills to overcome challenges and setbacks. Application of this will be detailed in later chapters, but we now have an understanding of how unhealthy confidence levels and artificial praise result in students' poor development and fear of failure. We must focus on supporting and encouraging students to strive for success, even in the face of failure, and offering them the pivotal skills needed to overcome these failures—or we will continue throwing our adolescents into a workforce and world they are not prepared for.

CHAPTER THREE

EFFECTS IN THE WORKPLACE

*"Confidence is directness and courage in meeting
the facts of life."*
—*John Dewey*

Have you ever worked with or managed co-workers who struggled to take logical next steps, even though they knew what those steps were? Did you wonder what skills they could have developed earlier in their lives to give them the ability (or confidence) to take those steps?

A few years back, I was mentoring a young teacher. This teacher was hired from a great undergraduate program and had a good base of content and educational theory. I remember working on a particular set of lessons with him about balancing chemistry equations. As we began, he constantly questioned what to do next and even asked me to write down the entire lesson with step-by-step instructions. Now, I do realize that new teachers need help applying their undergraduate program knowledge to implementation in the field...but this was different. He was so afraid to make a mistake that he just wanted me to give him detailed, line-itemized directions of exactly what to do and how. Really! He even wanted me to note when he should ask his class for questions and write on the board. I may as well have said, "Oh, also, let's make sure to indicate in the lesson plan that you shouldn't tell the students their questions are stupid." I could not believe it was an actual conversation.

When talking to other veteran teachers, this seemed not to be the exception to the rule, but rather a more common phenomenon with the younger generations. I was perplexed. What caused this? What experiences, or lack thereof, did this newer generation of individuals entering the workforce encounter as adolescents that caused them to develop this way?

I believe there is a new fear of failure from a lack of developing authentic confidence. The younger generations of the workforce have been overprotected, overpraised, and over-programed. They also entered their adolescent lives under the microscope of social media. No wonder they have a fear of failure...and request implicit directions from managers in order to avoid such failures. I have seen an increasing number of new teachers who fall under this category. I have also spoken with many managers and business-owners who complain of the same problem. The way we've raised children is hindering these next generations from being leaders in the workforce. Lack of authentic confidence can and will slow the opportunity for growing the leaders needed for tomorrow. This is a major concern and problem, and we need to address it—not just in our classrooms, but in other environments, as well.

How many articles have you seen or read about the Millennial Generation entering the workforce? "How to recruit Millennials." "How to manage Millennials." "How to retain Millennials." A quick article search from the first month of 2016 returned over 200 pieces written about Millennials in the workplace. To be fair, the Millennial Generation does seem to have a greater population that was exposed to parental and societal influences in regard to self-esteem and confidence, but the problem is not isolated just to them. It has existed for generations. We have seen similar behaviors exhibited by children who have an inflated sense of confidence and self-esteem just because of their parents' wealth. This is not always the case for children of wealthy individuals, as I have met many who were very appreciative and had authentic confidence, much in the same way I have met many Millennials who defy the current stigma surrounding them. Millennials also possess many redeeming characteristics which, when combined with authentic confidence, actually propel instead of hinder them. In every group and generation, you will see outliers who don't fit within the core group. However, stigmas exist for a reason—and in the case of Millennials, the stigma is supported by statistics, unfortunately.

We've previously identified why authentic confidence leads a child to develop a growth-centered mindset. These children can handle success with an appreciation for the work required to achieve such. They are also able to harvest failures for learning opportunities and identify skills to acquire in the process of overcoming those failures. But what happens when adolescents grow and enter the workforce without this authentic confidence? Are they at risk? Are they forced to mature and eventually grow out of it? If they lack this authentic confidence, what type of leaders do they become? Will they become leaders at all?

More than any other generation, the Millennials provide the clearest reason to support focusing on authentic confidence in children. In the next four years, Millennials born between 1977 and 1997 will account for nearly half of the employees in the world. In some companies, they already constitute a majority. Yet, organizations have had to turn their training and recruitment strategies upside down to accommodate both the good and challenging characteristics of Millennials. Thus, we have a fairly clear understanding of the cause and effect between classroom and extracurricular activities during adolescence with later development and growth in the workforce. We can certainly see these characteristics in other generations, too, but not quite as prominently. So, what characteristics define Millennials and others lacking authentic confidence?

Howe and Strauss (2003) from Rice University, among others, have defined some characteristics of the Millennial Generation. These characteristics can be used to show how this generation, more than others, lacks authentic confidence. Due to this, Millennials encounter more obstacles than necessary in workplace growth. Below are a few characteristics of Millennials as defined by Howe and Strauss (2003).

Sheltered:

Highly protected as children, they grew up in a time of increasing safety measures (car seats, baby on board signs, school lockdowns). They were rarely left unsupervised. They were sheltered from having to take care of their own conflicts, as parents advocated on their behalf and "spared" them from unpleasant experiences. As college students, they may expect faculty and staff to shelter, protect, and nurture them–and resolve their conflicts for them. Millennials are the focus of the most sweeping youth safety movement in American history.

Confident:

They may brag about their generation's power and potential. They have high levels of optimism and they feel connected to their parents. They are assertive and believe they are "right." In Canada, the Millennial generation is called the "Sunshine" generation.

Pressured:

Tightly scheduled as children, they are used to having every hour of their days filled with structured activity. This generation may have lost a sense of pure spontaneous play. They may struggle with handling free time and time management in general. In elementary, middle, and high school, they've had more hours of homework and less free time than any of the previous generations. They feel pressured to succeed. They've been pushed hard to achieve, to avoid risks, and to take advantage of opportunities. They may take on too much, and then think others should be flexible with them when they want to negotiate scheduling conflicts. They think multitasking saves time and is a smart thing to do but aren't usually aware of the poorer quality of results (p. 56-85).

Most Millennials have always been treated as "special" and "important." Each milestone was marked or awarded with celebrations and praise, whether it was deserved or not. With a sense of entitlement, they have an expectation of frequent positive feedback as a means to avoid failure—or at least limit it. One can easily see why this generation best exemplifies the lack of authentic confidence needed to embrace the challenges of tomorrow.

Managers today are challenged with coaching these young workers (who have built a particular reputation for being needy). Meister and Willyerd (2010) polled 2,200 professionals across a wide range of industries, asking about their Millennial employees' values, behavior at work, and wants from their employers. The survey confirmed that Millennials desired a constant stream of feedback and were in a hurry for success. They wanted praise for everything they did. Hershatter and Epstein (2010) say, "Millennials tend to lack the motivation in gathering information to seek a more nuanced one, and by failing to diligently follow a path of inquiry, they miss perspectives that would enable them to evaluate the analysis of others" (p. 3).

A lot of Millennials have always felt loved and wanted by overprotective parents, guided and cared for by teachers whose training focused on the importance of emotional and self-esteem building over realistic feedback. Generation X, who are acutely aware that life is not fair or easily played, tend to describe Millennials as "entitled." However, many Millennials view themselves as pressured and high-achieving, and they have grown accustomed to supportive, nurturing environments that provide them with every opportunity to succeed (Hershatter and Epstein, 2010). With such oversight and overbearing guidance, any ambiguity—or project or exam—requiring Millennials to work without guidelines is a challenge. They lack authentic confidence from years of over-praise and overprotection. They require templates or examples because they haven't practiced producing without clearly defined instructions and specific deadlines set by others.

Hershatter and Epstein (2010) hypothesize that this is also a result of legislation like the No Child Left Behind Act. They indicate that schools have frequently adjusted curricula and assessments to assure maximum success on standardized exams. This instruction model, coupled with parental demand for transparency in grading criteria, has meant that Millennials "expect very clearly outlined, objective rubrics and well-defined expectations" (Hershatter and Epstein, 2010, p. 216). Because they spent their childhoods receiving gold stars and shiny medals just for showing up, Millennials were indoctrinated from their earliest moments to seek approval and affirmation. Connecting the research from the previous chapter on inflated confidence, one can easily surmise that over-praise, coupled with a distorted view of accomplishment, has created a risk-averse, needy workforce.

In *The Trophy Kids Grow Up*, writer Ron Alsop (2008) of the

Wall Street Journal describes life's gray areas as some of these struggles Millennials face. Alsop also hints that leading employers report having to make specific accommodations to help Millennials wrestle with uncertainty and overcome aversion to risk-taking. Many have written stories disparaging the neediness, disloyalty, sense of entitlement, and overall casualness in Millennials' approaches to work. Charles and Gregory (2016) point out that this generation has been "shaped by, among other things, helicopter parents, frequent positive feedback and reassurance, significant leaps in technology, and political and economic turmoil" (p. 238). The Millennial Generation grew up with extraordinary levels of positive reinforcement and attention. They were praised and given inflated confidence and self-esteem, which has resulted in a lack of legitimate confidence. Parents and society focused on rewarding children for participation rather than performance, which coined these individuals as "trophy kids" (Alsop, 2008). As a result, society has latched on to this notion that Milllennials have a strong and unreasonable sense of entitlement (Deal, Altman, & Rogelberg, 2010).

This entitlement can be a strain in the workplace, as managers have to retool their mentoring and training programs to provide valuable and realistic feedback. This rearrangement has both delayed Millennials' abilities to advance in the workplace and also forced the workplace to, for the first time, conform to a generation rather than the generation conforming to it (Charles and Gregory, 2016). When combining praise for anything done, detailed instructions on how to do things, and an overprotected and scheduled adolescence, it's easy to foresee a lack of confidence in the face of challenges, either as a manager, employee, or even just as an adult.

Confidence is built when a person is challenged and overcomes that challenge through his or her own efforts. Young Millennials were faced with challenges, only to be told that their parents would take care of it or they would be rewarded even if they failed. So, we've told children they don't have to work hard, take risks, or organize themselves to get rewarded, and we've expected them to somehow develop a healthy sense of confidence to tackle life's challenges under these conditions. There is a tragic contradiction in this.

As we can see, the "I win, no matter what" attitude has negative effects in the workplace, specifically with Millennials. What about under-confidence, though? What are the effects of that in the workplace? Let's take a look at others who are sometimes challenged with confidence: women in the workplace.

There is research illustrating the challenge of low confidence in the workplace for some women. A KPMG survey of more than 3,000 women found that their perceptions of their leadership skills and seeds of self-doubt were planted in childhood (Toth, 2016). In the same survey, only one-third were encouraged to share their perspectives. At the 2015 Network of Executive Women (NEW) Leadership Summit, more than 1,200 women were inspired by female executives who overcame such doubts and became powerful and effective leaders. These high-powered women worked through their fears, sought the help of mentors and sponsors, and developed the confidence to challenge themselves, which broadened their skills and built their profiles. Kathy Russello, executive vice president of Ahold USA and panel contributor at the conference, shared how she was hesitant to take on a new role outside her area of expertise early in her career. She was given responsibility for labor relations strategy. She explained that she went into the role with a great deal of concern. However, through the experience, she learned the most because of the challenge (Toth, 2016).

What caused some women to lack confidence when facing certain challenges that some men seem to have no problem tackling? Deaux and Ennsuiller (1994) and Beyer and Bowden (1997) have noted that some women become less confident and more risk-averse in areas considered "masculine," despite their equal ability to perform. In these instances, women seem to exhibit several behaviors that exemplify this lack of confidence or over-confidence. Statistically speaking, women tend to be less likely to voice opinions and present unique ideas out of fear that their thoughts aren't good enough. Women also underestimate their abilities, making them less likely to apply for promotions and jobs, according to Shipman and Kay (2014). Women must be over-prepared and overqualified to feel adequate for a job, whereas men can be underprepared and under-qualified and will still apply for a job (Shipmen and Kay, 2014). Expectations that lead to reduced confidence in women are embedded in our societal norms. When we overprotect to the point of sheltering, we hinder individuals from experiences that build confidence.

This is evident in the historical societal expectation that girls should play with dolls and not participate in sports. Due to this, girls sometimes miss out on key confidence-building experiences and, in turn, more advanced careers. After the Title IX legislation, studies on girls' and boys' participation in school sports found that girls who play team sports are more likely to graduate from college and be employed in male-dominated industries. A correlation has been shown between playing sports in high school and earning a bigger salary as an adult (Shipman and Kay, 2014).

While sports is just one example, it is illustrative of how limiting childhood experiences leads to a lack of confidence and hurts future prospects in life. We see this more contemporarily in coding and engineering for girls. We have seen a surge in the amount of programming pushing to involve females in these areas. Why? Because we know that if they gain experience during adolescence in these disciplines, they will be more likely to have the confidence to not only be involved but also take risks and face challenges within these fields.

Jo Swinson, the past Parliamentary Under Secretary of State for Women and Equalities in the UK, said that a lack of confidence can act as a barrier to women achieving their full potential, and that's why governments are looking at ways to broaden the ambition and aspiration of girls in hopes of supporting them at all stages of their careers (McVeigh, 2013). According to a KPMG (2015) study, this lack of confidence in women affects an array of other activities "tied to ultimately becoming leaders: nine in 10 women said they do not feel confident asking for sponsors (92%), with large numbers also lacking confidence in seeking mentors (79%), asking for access to senior leadership (76%), pursuing a job opportunity beyond their experience (73%), asking for a career path plan (69%), requesting a promotion (65%), raise (61%), or a new role or position (56%)" (p. 5-6). The same study found that three in four (76%) women wish that they would have learned more about leadership and had more experiences to learn how to lead when they were growing up (75%). Furthermore, women with childhood leadership experience are more likely to be senior leaders today than those without that experience (KPMG, 2015). When those same women in the study were asked what else they thought led to their low confidence, they responded by saying that, in childhood, they were taught lessons that undermined an inclination to lead. They were told to practice the "golden rule" rather than be assertive or speak their minds. Two-thirds (65%) of women reported that when they were younger, they were hesitant to show they could be a leader (KPMG, 2015). They were not encouraged to challenge themselves and were not supported when they failed to find the skills that would eventually lead to success. Authentic confidence does not come from listening to motivational speeches, pep rallies, or just blind hope that it will be there when it is needed. It comes from a collection of experiences, both good and bad, that identify tools acquired and tools to-be-acquired to face challenges and obstacles.

Authentic confidence does not allow one to do absolutely everything. Authentically confident people have expectations that are realistic and understand that failure is possible. Even when they fail, they continue to be positive and accept failure as a learning experience. Challenges to our self-esteem and confidence are a part of everyday life. Learning how to overcome failure and negative experiences is key. While we can certainly learn this later in life, why wait? Self-confidence and positive self-esteem can and should be learned at early ages. While these experiences continue to shape our lives, seeing those experiences early on not only creates a growth-focused mindset, but enables adolescents and adults to face challenges and accept risks with minimal stress. The development of authentic confidence involves changes, new behaviors, and takes time and energy. It is not easy to teach children how to recognize failure or setbacks as positive learning moments. Building confidence depends on breaking old habits and developing new productive ones. Negative thinking is a natural human response and sometimes easier than focusing on positivity, especially during a stressful challenge. These thoughts can be so ingrained in our minds that we assume they cannot be changed, but they can.

The struggles of Millennials and women in workplaces illustrate the detrimental effects of ingrained behaviors and expectations. Learning how to acknowledge and deal with negative thoughts is an effective way to boost confidence and also self-esteem. We have to respect change and challenges. Having positive, problem-solving attitudes instead of negative, problem-generating ones will open opportunities rather than keep individuals stuck in a single place. By accepting change, we acknowledge that the world is always evolving and, to survive and thrive, we must evolve, too. We must develop a toolkit to call upon. When we focus on learning and positive thinking, our experiences turn into confidence.

It sounds like a great idea, but do people with this mindset really exist in the workplace? Yes. Serial entrepreneurs are great examples. They describe their past steps simply as pivots. They describe their companies as profitable learning centers for building experience rather than focusing on the drama of failures.

I remember the first time I worked for a serial entrepreneur. I was young and fresh out of my MBA program. I had worked for several years in the resort development industry, mostly in worldwide purchasing and logistics. He brought me on board to help him develop a hotel property. This entrepreneur had just launched a new product that combined the timeshare model with that of a traditional resort. One day, I sat with him to understand his story. He talked about living abroad and watching his family develop many businesses in Africa. He talked about the milk factories and hotels his family owned. He described his difficulty understanding why his father was involved in so many things. As he grew up, he felt the need to develop his own path and moved into the field of technology. It was not until later in life that he began his own development company. He slowly developed a portfolio of his own resorts in Greece. This is where, through trial and error, he developed his confidence to overcome and find ways to succeed.

I particularly remember a time when we were developing a small boutique hotel on South Beach in Miami, Florida. We had a major investor who was working closely with us to provide the capital for the renovations—with the hope to launch a revitalization of what is now considered the north end of South Beach. One morning, I woke up and turned on the news, as I usually did while getting ready for the workday. The big news was that our major investor and prominent businessman had passed away unexpectedly the night before. I immediately called my CEO, the entrepreneur, and asked if he had seen the morning headlines. Unfortunately, he had not. The next few days were trying, to say the least, as we scrambled to save the project. When I asked the entrepreneur if we should just shut down the project, he told me that it was a test, a lesson that would provide dividends in the future in several ways. First, he said it taught us to not rely on a single investor. Second, he said if we failed and had to shut down the project, we would learn many other things—including, obviously, how to close a project. His confidence in the lessons of the experience confused me at first. Then I realized that his mindset was actually a reflection of his authentic confidence with handling failure in a positive and productive manner. He saw the failure as just part of his learning and preparation for his next project.

Successful entrepreneurs learn from their mistakes and then use that insight as operational wisdom for thriving on future projects. Very rarely do you see a serial entrepreneur whose portfolio shows only successes. The most important piece is that they use their experience and confidence to find ways to hedge future projects. Serial entrepreneurs possess a solid dose of authentic confidence, the kind that shields from self-doubt and makes one impervious to pessimistic thoughts, even if the path taken doesn't work sometimes. The bottom line is that we need authentic confidence to be a Bill Gates, Henry Kaiser, or Ted Turner. We have to be able to see each and every opportunity as a learning moment and use that learning as a springboard for achievement.

The ability to develop authentic confidence in adolescents is a key component for future success. It is only one spoke in the wheel on that road (although I would argue it's at least a few spokes). Regardless, it's a very critical one to have in the toolbox. And while there are many people who are creating their own successes and succeeding, some are playing catch-up in developing the confidence to challenge themselves and take risks. Authentic confidence in the workplace and adult life is essential. Now, imagine if we were able to provide more structure in our classrooms and children's extracurricular activities for experiences that built authentic confidence. From this, adolescents could stand up and stand out. We need them to acquire this growth-based mindset and use authentic confidence to take those next steps. Learning from experiences is one thing...but learning from experiences and then applying those skills to a new situation, challenge, or leap of faith takes authentic confidence. So how do we do that? How do we structure our world to provide experiences that grow our children's authentic confidence?

CHAPTER FOUR

PROBLEMS IN THE CLASSROOM

"He who is not courageous enough to take risks will
accomplish nothing in life."
—*Muhammed Ali*

As a teacher, administrator, or parent observing today's educational policies and lack of concern for individuals, one might be worried or even scared about the state of education in our country. Have you wondered why students take certain tests or focus on certain subjects or ideas that just seem to hinder their progress? These feelings are not unfounded, and you certainly are not alone, whether you're a teacher, parent, or an everyday observer. Instructional and testing initiatives have been implemented that do nothing but stall progress, deflate children's self-esteem and confidence, and create problems rather than solve them.

I remember talking to a fellow teacher in the public schools of Miami-Dade County, Florida. She explained that the underlying message being sent to teachers was to focus on getting their students to pass the state exam. This was a priority because it was necessary for federal funding, and that funding provided resources for teachers to do their jobs. Oh, also, teachers had to do this year after year, so their primary focuses were continually getting a new bunch of students to pass the exam. And another thing: teachers would be given salary raises or bonuses based on how many of their children passed the exams. I remember asking her how this made her feel. She exhaled a long sigh, and then a tear ran down her face. She said that she did not have a choice and, unfortunately, would need to focus on the exam. She needed her job, she explained, but she knew this was not what teaching was about. She added that many teachers felt the same way, but just did what they had to do, which did not include building students' skills and strengths for future successes.

In a 2015 Op-Ed *Baltimore Sun* editorial piece by Anne Groth, she writes about why teachers are leaving their professions. She explains that teachers leave, not because they cannot teach, but because they are not allowed to. Groth (2015) goes on to say that "the testing and the pressure to get the students ready to do well on the tests leaves little time for real teaching and learning. In many districts across the country, student test scores are used to evaluate teachers without any solid evidence that the tests are valid indicators of real learning" (p. 13). Teachers want to work with kids and build their skills and confidence. Teachers are leaving because they are exhausted from implementing new curriculums or programs every year, which are, according to Groth, "always touted as 'research based,' but upon further scrutiny, the research is elusive, flawed or just non-existent" (p. 13). The classroom is not a science experiment and is too often the place where people want outside world problems to be fixed. Groth (2015) adds, "Teachers leave because they feel that they have failed, and they take with them all their talents, creativity, and dedication. Teachers leave because they have lost their confidence" (p. 13). If we are trying to build confidence in our children, we also have to take notice of our teachers' confidence in their abilities to teach and reach our students.

What happened to focusing on the students, their individual growth, and preparing their life skills? I think the last standardized test I had to take was in college. I cannot remember taking one to get my current job, or the one before that, or even before that. Testing is just one broad initiative that has helped raise the wall that separates students from their genuine confidence.

Other areas of concern include that of rigor and educators teaching primarily to the bottom third (rather than each individual). Authentic confidence faces an uphill battle unless we remove some of these barriers.

A colleague of mine used an analogy for this. He said whether we are administrators or teachers in private or public schools in the suburbs or the city, the process of educating students is like snow. If you have shoveled snow before, you know the difference between light fluffy snow, and heavy wet snow. Both are still snow, but one definitely takes more effort. What some of these national initiatives are doing to education is dampening and weighing down the snow. The process of building authentic confidence in adolescents should be like shoveling light snow—not heavy snow. If we are to truly ignite the passion and skills of our students, we have to lighten the snow.

I have already alluded to the fact that standardized testing is a huge obstacle for our teachers and students. Our approach is all wrong. Do not misunderstand me—I am not entirely opposed to standardized assessment, as I think it should play a role, but certainly not the role it is currently playing. Standards and assessments are important for diagnostic purposes. However, too often the data produced by standardized tests is not made available to teachers until after the school year ends. The timing doesn't provide the necessary feedback; end-of-the-year data delivery makes it impossible to use the information to address student needs. When tests are used in this way, they do little more than just measure predictable inequities in academic outcomes. Students have the right to see concrete evidence that they are learning, but standardized tests do not currently provide this evidence. How can children learn what they have done wrong, identify the missing skill with help from a teacher, acquire that skill, and then overcome the challenge if they don't even know what they did wrong? And sometimes, even if they do find out, it is too little or too late. We are giving them a score that either says, "You did well," or, "You did not do well, so...oh, well." The child then must emotionally develop a coping mechanism because an authoritative figure (a school, state government, or federal government) said he or she was a failure. This system is slowly destroying students' chances to have any confidence.

For the past two decades, the trend in federal, state, and local educational policy circles has been to require more standardized exams to establish common achievement benchmarks and hold schools accountable for student progress. Lowered academic self-concept is one consequence of underachievement on high-stakes tests.

Academic self-concept is considered a wide construct, reflecting both descriptive and evaluative aspects of the self (Altshuler and Schmautz, 2016). The relationship between academic self-concept and academic achievement is mostly reciprocal (Marsh, 1990). To put it simply, positive self-concept in adolescents fosters achievement, and successful achievement strengthens self-concept. However, negative academic self-concept has a limiting effect on academic achievement (Altshuler and Schmautz, 2016). For instance, research has found significant relationships between academic self-concept and school withdrawal (House, 1996). In order for a child to build a foundation for future success, his or her academic self-concept must be positive. An adolescent does not develop positive self-concept by simply receiving standardized test scores that offer nothing beyond, "You failed," or, "You are failing."

A study of adolescents in a Los Angeles county high school by Buriel et al. (1998) found that a number of these children had disparately low outcomes on such standardized assessments. Buriel et al. found that when these students faced a repeated lack of success on these standardized assessments throughout the school year, they exhibited lowered self-efficacy. Students who performed poorly on the standardized assessments and were not given the tools to evaluate, reflect, and correct their skills experienced years of poor performance and low self-esteem. Reduced academic self-concept and perception of confidence may culminate in elevated levels of frustration, loss of interest in academics, and disbelief in the reality of lifetime achievement through education (Altshuler and Schmautz, 2016). By focusing solely on the outcome instead of how to correct or improve that outcome, we are setting students up to enter higher education and life with a lack of confidence and self-esteem.

According to Williams (2003), self-concept serves as an important factor that influences economic success and long-term health and well-being. Adolescents' desire for authentic confidence in themselves and its benefits regarding choices, planning, persistence, and subsequent accomplishments are also well-documented through research (Marsh, Craven, & Mcinerney, 2003, 2005; Mcinerney, Marsh, & Craven, 2008). Standardized testing, along with other educational initiatives limiting teachers' encouraging positive self-concept in their students, are hurting the future abilities of our adolescents. This not only has an academic effect, but social and emotional consequences, as well.

Mcinerney et al. (2016) describe the academic element as divided into self-concepts specific to school subjects, such as English, science, and mathematics. The nonacademic component is divided into physical, social, and emotional components. It is important to understand that teachers affect students' academic and non-academic self-concepts equally. This is important in preparation for the working world, but it also has implications in higher education. Research has shown that many first-year college and university students experience a wide range of problems as a result of not adjusting to their new roles (Beyers & Goossens, 2002; Buote et al., 2007). Consequently, many students prematurely drop out of college. It is well-known among universities and colleges that the freshman dropout rate is significant. Colleges and universities have invested heavily into the freshman experience and support as a result. However, I think it better to address students' pre-college educational issues, since that is where the roots of the problems lie. Previous research has already identified self-concept or confidence as a significant positive predictor of academic adjustment in higher education (Mooney, Sherman, & Lopresto, 1991; Napoli & Wortman, 1998). Wouters et al. (2016) demonstrated in a study that students with better academic self-concept in high school tend to be more successful in coping with the new academic demands of higher education. As one can probably guess, students have higher chances of succeeding in their first year of higher education when they enter with positive self-concepts and higher confidence levels (Dickha et al., 2005; Durik et al., 2006; Lent et al., 2000; Lindley, 2005). The link between success in higher education and confidence levels is clear. This plethora of standardized testing has damaged our students' abilities to be confident in both current and higher levels of education. The need for test scores has outweighed the need for real teaching.

Over-testing is certainly a culprit and is definitely putting strain on confidence, as we can see in the rise in anxiety in children. One projective study found that students overwhelmingly felt stress, anxiety, worry, and isolation as a result of testing (Triplett & Barksdale, 2005). Segool et al. (2013) found that students felt significantly more test anxiety in relation to the high-stakes NCLB assessment than to everyday classroom tests. The following chart from this Segool et al. (2013) study shows just how much.

Test Anxiety Among School Children

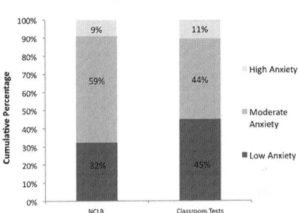

A significantly greater number of children feel moderate to high anxiety as a result of high-stakes standardized testing than ever before. It's predicted that this percentage will only continue growing if we keep focusing on standardized tests as a primary data-gathering tool and the focus of teacher evaluation and compensation. The amount of testing in our classrooms is clearly causing psychological side-effects that seem to be reaching unprecedented levels. The Segool et al. study findings are consistent with other studies examining teachers' perceptions of the impacts of high-stakes testing on children. Also, Segool et al. (2013) found that teachers were reporting that they experienced "significantly more anxiety about their students' performance on the NCLB assessment than on classroom testing. Specifically, teachers were more likely to worry about how well their students would perform on high-stakes tests compared with regular classroom tests" (p. 496). This observation may have important implications for students' confidence, because research has shown that when teachers experience increased anxiety, stress, and pressure, they change their instructional patterns to focus on test preparation (Abrams et al., 2003). The problem is only being compounded each year by this continual focus on high-stakes standardized testing or even just multiple yearly standardized tests.

The clinical world of psychology has established that anxiety erodes the confidence of individuals. Tests do have their place and play a part in painting a picture of an adolescent's performance. However, current methods of delivery and the frequency of that delivery are doing nothing to improve our students' abilities to tackle and challenge existing and future obstacles.

Class size is another damaging factor in current learning environments. More and more children are being placed in each classroom due to short-term financial hurdles faced by schools and districts, causing long-term effects on students' development and learning. Classrooms are busting at the seams in many areas of the country. Two years ago, a report from NEA Today discussed how schools in Georgia, in the midst of major funding cuts, had no choice but to lift all class-size limitations to accommodate students with the faculty they could still afford to keep (Flannery, 2016). Recently, Fairfax County in Virginia has been looking into a proposal to increase classroom sizes in the face of significant budget cuts—and some classrooms will exceed thirty-five students (Shapiro, 2014). The Board of Education in South Carolina is also weighing options in this area due to a current battle over funding (Chen, 2015). When money gets tight, classroom numbers are often impacted.

A majority of teachers agree that they cannot effectively teach each student in a classroom if the class size exceeds about 25 pupils. Research on class size performed by Tennessee's STAR Project found that classes of 15 to 17 students in grades K-3 provided both long- and short-term benefits for both students and teachers (Hosteler, 2008). Minority, impoverished, and male students appeared to benefit from smaller classroom sizes the most. It seems obvious to many teachers and parents that class size is an important factor in learning quality and the development of confidence. Research has also shown that class size effects progress in literacy and mathematics (Blatchford, 2003, p. 121). While many factors contribute to learning outcomes in adolescents within a classroom, teachers continuously note that they cannot reach all students because of current classroom sizes. Thus, this minimal opportunity to provide supportive and engaging feedback during class time is a huge challenge to building authentic confidence in adolescents. Teachers have to be able to spend time helping students navigate the challenges they face.

Galton et al. (1999) investigated teachers in larger classes. They saw teachers in these classes reducing the length of curriculum interactions via reduced direct student engagement and by offering briefer, more summative feedback. Both of these strategies for handling larger class sizes are counterproductive to confidence development. The greater impacts of large class sizes can been seen in students' struggles later in life. Importantly, small classes have been found to have positive impacts, not only on test scores, but also on life outcomes (Schanzenbach, 2014).

Frediksson et al. (2013) evaluated the longterm impacts of class size using data from students in Sweden between ages ten and thirteen. At age thirteen, students in smaller classes showed higher cognitive and non-cognitive skills, such as effort, motivation, and authentic confidence. In adulthood (between ages 27 and 42), those who had been in smaller classes had higher levels of completed education, wages, and earnings (Frediksson et al., 2013). Recent studies clearly show that overcrowding classrooms is inciting adverse effects on a majority of our adolescents' life preparation. Their abilities to gain confidence for handling life situations are being impaired and slowed. Schanzenbach (2014) even suggests that "increasing class size will harm not only children's test scores in the short run but also their long-term human capital formation. Money saved today by increasing class sizes will be offset by more substantial social and educational costs in the future" (p. 10).

If we are going to accept the rationale that larger class sizes are acceptable, even while a great number of students in these classes are floundering in under-performance, then we must also accept that our workforce will be ill-prepared to handle the challenges and needs of companies in the near future. Industries will need to invest time and effort to train and develop the confidence of their employees, which will inevitably lead to a delay in economic growth. Small—or even reasonable—class sizes are imperative to building authentic confidence in children. Small class sizes make real teaching possible. Children will not simply be a number. They will be seated around a table with their teacher, who can guide them in analysis, discussion, debate, presentation skills, opinions, and research, which all lead to building confidence in their learning experiences.

Many educators are turning to technology to help solve the problems they are facing in the classroom. For some, technology is a helping hand, and one that can provide individual help for each student, as it is easily custom-tailored. Technology is essential in classrooms for keeping up with the learning demands of the 21st century. Unfortunately, schools that are already struggling financially are increasing class sizes in order to integrate computers and other forms of technology in their classes. Technology will hopefully offset larger class sizes and be cheaper on a per-pupil basis in the long run. Educational companies are jumping in and seeing billions in investments in "EdTech" (educational technology) by offering school districts packages and discounts—and even asking corporations and foundations for "big gifts" (like going to the government for the funding). Technology is being used to replace teachers. Whether it is a flipped classroom (when students read course content at home and do homework in class the next day) or an online class, students are being asked to learn the content online through a tutorial or video and then come to class with questions. This has turned the teacher into more of a "problem solver" than an actual instructor. It is still true that technology has its place in the classroom and is a huge resource for support and enhancing the delivery of content and curricula. It is not a teacher, though, and shouldn't be the sole deliverer of lessons and lectures. Students inherently have questions, and part of being a great teacher is recognizing when a student may be struggling with a subject or particular concept—something a computer cannot do. I have always said that teachers are also part-time psychologists and sociologists. Teachers can intentionally call on students who fear answering or avoid opportunities to engage to build upon these students' learning experiences. Delivering content entirely online leaves a void of understanding and interaction which the teacher cannot explore.

Lectures are an effective way to help students acquire new knowledge (Hattie, 2008). Research has shown that having teachers who recognize and respond to students' social and emotional needs is just as important to academic development as specific instructional practices (Hamre & Pianta, 2005). You cannot do that if your students are at home studying the content.

Being able to respond to students' needs on an individual basis and in an immediate way helps provide support when they struggle. Increased opportunities for feedback improve student learning because feedback has one of the strongest effects of any instructional practice (Beesley & Apthorp, 2010; Hattie, 2008). Using technology in the classroom alongside lectures and immediate feedback is generally a good practice, and one form of flipped classrooms that has initial support in research for building academic self-confidence. However, if the teacher is unable to circulate and engage with all the students, then academic self-confidence begins to slip as frustrations with learning the material set in.

Schools provide numerous opportunities for children to measure themselves against others in terms of intelligence, physical skills, and popularity. This measurement can have both positive and negative effects on self-image. Adolescents will see themselves as incapable, thus eroding their confidence when faced with what seem to be, in their eyes, insurmountable challenges. However, when a teacher is there to help and provide that support at that critical time, the student can build a confident framework for overcoming that challenge. Technology can certainly help with that, but it can also be a downfall if not utilized in a manner that supports building a student's confidence.

Another challenge with technology in the classroom is that teachers may lack the level of engagement with technology most adolescents are used to. A student's love of technology tends to distract him from his schoolwork, which is simple and less interactive than other games, according to NEA Today (NEA Today, 2010). Most teachers aren't techno-savvy enough to compete with those programs. It can be difficult to keep students' interest and attention and properly teach new concepts. Teachers just cannot keep up with Hollywood and the gaming industry enough to effectively combine engaging technology with content delivery. There are EdTech firms that are trying to do this, and progress is being made, especially in early childhood development. However, as we progress through the grade levels, fewer and fewer teachers are able to utilize technology in an interactive and highly engaging way to deliver curriculum. The result is students losing interest—especially when the classroom technology is antiquated in the eyes of the youngsters.

The greater challenge is expanding teachers' knowledge of new instructional practices that will allow them to select and use the right technologies, in the right ways, with the right students, for the right purposes. We have thrown technology into classrooms because many consider it a saving grace in providing individualized instruction in overcrowded settings. The problem is that teachers are overwhelmed and undereducated in the use and identification of proper EdTech technologies. This leads to students being left to comprehend and understand content on their own, which is a recipe for disaster in terms of building their confidence.

There are so many different areas in which educators continue to erode students' authentic confidence. Whether it be over-testing, the overcrowding of classrooms, or the improper use of technology, classrooms are creating problems of epidemic proportions that are leading to a restructuring of many companies and organizational HR departments. These classroom issues are leading to students needing to be spoon-fed information and organized lists with directions. The ability of a student to think on his or her own and tackle a problem without direction is becoming an unusual trait. This proves that our educational system is failing to properly teach critical thinking. This is also why we are lagging, as a nation, in student achievement in science and math—two subjects that require critical thinking, challenges, and the need to learn from failure. We have to give teachers the skills necessary to build authentic confidence in students. Without such, our students won't have the mental and emotional stamina to overcome greater obstacles in life. It is essential that teachers be skilled in seeing and embracing the potential of each of their students. It is essential that a child has moments of realization and symbolically yells, "Eureka!" It is in this that the building blocks of authentic confidence are placed, and they can then move on to the next challenge. Teaching children how to cope with challenges, think critically, synthesize information, and solve problems are the building blocks of authentic confidence...and authentic confidence is the foundation of successful, capable, and motivated adults.

PART TWO

A CONFIDENT FUTURE

<u>CHAPTER FIVE</u>

BUILDING CONFIDENCE IN THE CLASSROOM

"Do not be embarrassed by your failures; learn from them and start again."
—Richard Branson

We have talked at length about the obstacles that lower or hinder confidence levels in children. But what happens when we build confidence in the classroom? What does that look like, and what can teachers and administrators do to establish authentic confidence in each child? I believe that our teachers know confidence when they see it, but it does not come easily—and it takes substantial effort from both the teacher and the student. If it were easy, I would not be writing this book to start a conversation about it.

I've had to think hard about when I first felt authentic confidence building in myself. I've thought back to grade school and even high school. I am sure that I had some moments. I certainly remember instances in which I felt myself building this true confidence when I played sports or interacted in the community, but I will share those experiences in the next chapter.

The first time I remember genuinely feeling academic authentic confidence was actually in college. Believe it or not, I was in organic chemistry, of all classes. My professor at the University of Miami was considered one of the toughest in his department. The class was designed to weed out those students who were seeking careers in chemistry or medicine. I remember sitting in the lecture hall with eighty fellow students, a group much smaller than my inorganic chemistry class the semester prior. We were studying the structure of molecules, and we'd been asked in the classroom material list to get model kits of different elements to form compounds. We were working on the formation of molecules and bonds—some of which were very difficult. We were told that during the exam we would be able to use our molecule kits, but we were not allowed additional time on the exam.

As we began to work on the models, I struggled to figure out the placements of bonds. Which electrons were shared? How did the positive or negative charge of a molecule affect its ability to combine with other molecules? For those who took organic chemistry, I am sure this brings back memories.

There was then a key moment for me when the struggling suddenly stopped, and the three-dimensional molecule came to life. Looking back to my childhood, I thought of all those years playing Legos and having to find the hidden piece in the bottom of the drawer. I would dig and dig, knowing it was there somewhere among the hundreds of other pieces. Once the piece was found, then came making it fit in a way that completed the build. The molecules were just like Lego puzzles. I began to figure them out and developed speed and confidence in my ability to tackle difficult and sometimes nearly impossible combinations. I did not feel fear, and I developed the authentic confidence to solve any problem, regardless of its difficulty, by trusting in my capability to figure it out. What did my professor have to do with this building of confidence? He never stopped raising the bar and challenged me at every turn. It was hard and sometimes frustrating, but he assured us that there was a solution if we just looked hard enough.

I hope that each of us has experienced such a moment in our

academic careers. If we look back to our favorite teachers—the ones who seem to hold special places in our hearts—we will begin to recognize that those are the people who helped build our authentic confidence. They may be those teachers who pushed you, those you actually thought were too hard on you...but they saw something more in you than you did. Building authentic confidence in children is hard and takes time and effort, but the payoff is huge. Our future as a country and global community is dependent upon it. So—what can teachers do to build authentic confidence in the classroom?

One crucial action educators can take is to challenge their students.

I have met a lot of teachers in my career, as well as a lot of professionals in the world of business. Many teachers say they challenge students in their classrooms daily. However, I have found that many business leaders see a lack of employees challenging themselves in the working world, which would contradict teachers' perceived classroom experiences. In 1983, the report titled "A Nation at Risk: The Imperative for Educational Reform" called for more rigor (not challenge) in our schools. The glossary of education reform explains that while "dictionaries define the term as rigid, inflexible, or unyielding, educators frequently apply rigor or rigorous to assignments that encourage students to think critically, creatively, and more flexibly. Likewise, they may use the term rigorous to describe learning environments that are not intended to be harsh, rigid, or overly prescriptive, but that are stimulating, engaging, and supportive" (Hidden Curriculum, 2014, p. 1).

How we instill these characteristics varies widely and depends on several factors. Although most teachers claim they challenge their students, I would argue instead that they have rigor, which is represented in the school and the curriculum. When we challenge students, we are talking about student readiness and task completion—and that is different from educational rigor. Many educators confuse and intermingle these two concepts.

Educators also tend to confuse difficulty with complexity. When we talk about challenging our students, we're talking about complexity more than difficulty. Complexity relates to the kind of thinking, action, and knowledge needed in order to answer a question, solve a problem, or complete a task. It also looks at how many different ways there are to perform or solve these tasks. Complex questions, problems, and tasks often challenge and engage students in different ways. They have to rely on their experiences and sometimes take risks to complete the tasks. Students solving complex problems tend to think at the higher levels of Bloom's Taxonomy and communicate strategic and extended thinking. For those who are unfamiliar, Bloom's Taxonomy is a strategy for organizing and assorting academic-based goals, as developed by Benjamin Bloom (with the aid of Edward Furst, David Krathwohl, Max Englehart, and Walter Hill). They examined and categorized six learning process abilities, which they labeled Knowledge, Comprehension, Application, Analysis, Synthesis, and Evaluation. Knowledge was the necessary precondition for putting these skills and abilities into practice (Longman, 2001).

Complex problems and tasks allow students to delve deeper into the content, concepts, ideas, subjects, and topics being learned. Challenging and complex problems engage students to establish and examine relationships, explore causes and effects, and consider options and possibilities. A great example of how this is done in the classroom is through the use of Singapore Math. Originally developed in Singapore, Singapore Math aims to teach students how to learn and master fewer mathematical concepts in greater detail through a three-step learning process (Brown, 2016). It is used widely today by many schools and has been adopted by many districts as the standardized math program for all students.

With these two educational strategies in mind, let's look at some word problems in a few different formats.

Difficult but simple:

Jane has 10 cookies and Joe has 12; how many do they have altogether?

Hard:

Jessica and Lillian had the same amount of money. Jessica gave $1,140 to a charity, and Lillian gave $580 to a different charity. In the end, Lillian had nine times as much money as Jessica. How much money did each girl have at first?

Complex:

Jane had $7 and her sister had $2. Their parents gave them each an equal amount of money. Then Jane had twice as much money as her sister. How much money did their parents give each of them?

In order to instill challenge in classrooms, a teacher should use these three styles of word problems according to the ability of each individual child. Too many educators stop at the first or second question because it alone would demonstrate "mastery" of the concept. This is where we go wrong in building authentic confidence. For some children, the first question could be a challenge and thus an opportunity to build authentic confidence. However, this is where the trouble begins. Due to testing requirements and essential content for standardized tests, teachers are quickly covering content to check a box rather than creating a challenging academic environment for each student. This is an example of teaching to the bottom third: the top two-thirds would master the concept quickly or independently, but it's the bottom third's performance that would determine whether a school meets state and national standards. Unfortunately, it is the upper two-thirds of the classroom that would miss out on the opportunity to be challenged and develop confidence.

Challenging students also requires engaging them in what is being taught and how it is delivered. Some teachers say that certain students just do not like certain subjects. Through being involved in education for some time now, I would argue instead that we just haven't engaged these students correctly or challenged them in that subject—not that they don't have an affinity towards certain subjects. I believe that upon entering higher education and maybe even during the last years of high school, a student tends to develop interests in specific subjects. But prior to those years, if educators engage students correctly and challenge them, pupils will take interest in almost all subjects. We want teachers to pose questions, present problems, and provide tasks that are more complex than difficult—which, in turn, will aid in building genuine confidence. Where and when to provide more complex problems depends on what exactly our students need to know and understand. Students need to be able to demonstrate and communicate their knowledge, understanding, and thinking, because this helps build academic confidence in a meaningful and authentic manner.

Another key ingredient to building authentic academic confidence is making sure students understand the qualitative, real-world applications of what they are learning. Pulling again from my own personal experience, I remember my geometry teacher, who granted me an amazing academic experience. She consistently held the bar high and challenged me. She was always there for support, but that bar never lowered. Both our textbook and teacher gave several examples of real-life applications—but not to the extent that it made me believe I would ever use geometry in the outside world. We covered more on the overall existence of geometrical figures rather than their everyday applications. This was a missing piece that caused a gap in my educational experience, even though my memories of my teacher were memorable and positive.

I didn't develop authentic confidence in the use of geometric rules until I was in my mid-twenties. Prior to working in education, I had a job in hotel development. I remember I was renovating a hotel on South Beach, Florida. It was an art deco hotel with 60 rooms on the north end of South Beach. We were required to upgrade the doors and entries to accommodate standards for the ADA (Americans with Disabilities Act of 1990). This meant expanding existing doors from 32 inches to 36 inches. However, due to furniture placement and roof-supporting pillars in the hallways, we could not just increase the widths of the doors in the hallways. Along came my geometric principles to save the day and provide the long-overdue confidence needed in this subject area. Thank you to my geometry teacher for drilling concepts into my head so I could recall it in this situation. Using the Pythagorean Theorem, with one side (jamb) being 36 inches and the other 32 inches, I determined the length of the last side and how I needed to angle the new doors. This is an example of what we need to use when working with students so they see qualitative, real-world applications. It provides confidence in that the material being presented is, in fact, usable. By the way—the new hallways turned out beautifully with my adjustments. They had visually pleasing wave-like patterns.

Let's analyze another everyday school subject: history. Many students and teachers wonder what real-life application can be connected to historical events. My father, a history major at Emory University, used to tell me that history has a tendency to repeat itself, and he'd even provide examples. Why does it repeat itself, and how can we engage students to think about this? It is rare to find a teacher who takes history and maps the decisions and events of different eras to examine similarities and outcomes through cross-analysis and utilizing tactics like decision trees. I know students would fully engage with such a project due to its challenging complexity.

The business consultant and author Jim Collins compared different companies that succeeded or failed when given the same opportunities. Could we not engage students with the same logic and research by applying historical economical, humanitarian, and political situations to current ones and then discuss how they relate? Again, I am sure that students would be very interested in this kind of application.

Another example of real-world application comes from a recent road trip I took from Wisconsin to Florida. Yes, I was escaping winter for my children's spring break. Anyway, as we passed trucks along the road, my wife and I began to recognize that certain trucks had what was called TrailerTail. We wondered why so many trucks had this device. After some quick internet research, we found out that the TrailerTail created a more aerodynamic truck and increased overall fuel efficiency by 5.5%. My past physics classes and the importance of aerodynamic formulas suddenly made sense—I could see the principles in action. I wish my teacher had used such an example when teaching aerodynamics, as it would've given me a more realistic grasp and confidence in the principles I was studying.

The development of authentic confidence in children requires real-life application that students can relate to. If educators offer such, children will begin operating at the highest levels of Bloom's Taxonomy through analyzing, evaluating, and creating. What if, in a subject (whether it be English, history, science, or math), teachers challenged their students to go out into the world and find examples of the content they are being taught? Then, they could come back, share those examples with the class, and, in turn, possibly imagine and create an ideal environment or concept from all the combined examples. This would fully utilize Bloom's Taxonomy with challenge and real-world application.

Another component of building authentic confidence in the classroom is resilience. How do students respond to new challenges? Do they respond with confidence and flexibility? Are they clear about what they want to achieve from challenges? Are they good at utilizing alternative resources, such as friends, parents, or teachers? Are they reaching out for support when they're overwhelmed by mounting academic pressure? The answers to these questions can illustrate what students with resilience look like.

Hayter and Heathcock (2011) say that purposefulness, adaptability, and social support are key components of developing resilience. Students need to be able to adapt to uncertainty and different challenges. Children who are able to adapt are less likely to feel overwhelmed or helpless. When we think about the future and the increasing speed of the world, change is the new constant—and if students are to feel confident, they must be able to adapt. They also need to have the social support of teachers and classmates to fully develop the confidence needed for future life situations they may encounter. These days, we all know that the ability to call upon others for expertise or help is essential in life.

Confidence also requires knowing that one can find and access these resources. Finally, students gain a sense of purposefulness when they develop a natural drive to do better and push further. Helping students see the bigger picture for why they should want to do better in school, dive deeper into a subject, and know the reasoning behind a concept (rather than just the concept itself) helps build purposefulness.

It is vital that classrooms provide an environment in which students can explore the skills that create resilience. It takes time and trust to develop, but is yet another essential in building the foundation for authentic confidence. Teachers need to focus on several aspects of building academic resilience, know when to intervene, and provide supportive feedback and encouragement. A clear illustration occurs when students experience something academically negative, like a poor evaluation or grade on an assignment or task. They may say or display an attitude of, "I'm a failure," or, "I have to succeed because my teacher, mom, or dad will be disappointed and not respect me." Catching and dealing with these fleeting thoughts can be difficult for teachers and parents alike, but taking the time to recognize the signs can help provide a critical intervention to protect the student's resilience. Signs include things like a slouching head or a quick turning-over of the evaluation or grade to avoid facing the disappointment. There are probably more signs that behavioral psychologists could certainly identify, but as an educator, I can tell when students are disappointed. Providing an encouraging comment or helping identify a path to improvement will help to build resilience and confidence. Teachers should also build upon successes...not by just saying, "You're good at this, so keep going," but by identifying the specific skills the child exhibited to succeed and encouraging the use of those skills in future challenges. Did the student study hard, or did he or she use flashcards or mnemonics (memory development techniques)? Identify the skills used and encourage their usage in other academic areas to help build upon successes.

Resilience is tough because outside environments play a key role in helping it develop in the classroom. However, the building of resilience in the classroom can deliver results outside the classroom, as well. It is important that students know that in times of challenge, friends, parents, teachers, and others can be sources of reassurance that provide helpful feedback and perspective.

I have seen this in action time and time again during the college application and acceptance process. Students all over the United States become disenfranchised and depressed when they do not get into the colleges of their choice. They have failed to develop the resilience to handle that, even though they wanted to fly to Europe, the plan dropped them in Tennessee. Resilience allows them to see the opportunities they can have and experience in that moment (rather than focusing on what they did not get). Resilience is a key attribute to have and work on when developing authentic confidence.

Teachers also need to provide an environment where students can take risks. Such an environment can be scary for pupils, but it provides the greatest opportunity to build authentic confidence. How do we provide opportunities for students to face risks within the classroom? How can a student take a risk in English, or even history? First, we have to understand what each particular student struggles with in order to create an environment where they will take a risk. For example: I was in third grade when I was asked to give a presentation in front of my classmates. I was a quiet kid and did not have the confidence to present academically in front of the class. I was in a new school that year and was still trying to find my place. My teacher knew this was a real struggle for me, but she challenged me to take the risk and present. I remember her giving me some advice on how to handle the fear, like curling my toes in my shoes. When I completed my presentation and the students applauded, I felt a sense of accomplishment I had never felt before. My confidence foundation was gaining bricks. Now, there were several presentations that day, and my fellow students applauded for everyone. However, I had a fear (and thus a risk) that they would not have clapped for me. Having my teacher's support through the risk helped me build the authentic confidence I use today to present in front of hundreds of people.

You see, just because a student trusts a teacher doesn't mean he or she necessarily trusts everyone else in the classroom. In order for students to develop confidence, they need to take emotional and intellectual risks in front of peers and other teachers. Creating and providing opportunities for those emotional and intellectual risks in a monitored environment is essential for developing authentic confidence. The environment needs to facilitate tough challenges while simultaneously teaching students not to give up when they face adversity or even failure. I am not talking about putting kids at emotional or physical risk that could cause long-term detrimental harm. I am talking about the little successes and failures that create learning moments for each student. If a teacher can guide them through those learning moments, students can begin to develop authentic confidence productively. The challenge for teachers, on the other hand, is to not falsely inflate the student's ego, but to supportively and realistically explain to the child what happened and what to do to overcome similar obstacles in the future.

I believe that due to time constraints and checklists for common core or other promised fixes, teachers have little time to work with students through these problems. But if they could, I'd expect that teachers would question students' answers and challenge them to go back and try again, rather than just saying, "You got it wrong," and giving them the solution. Part of developing authentic confidence is learning to take risks and gaining from them. Teachers can develop reward systems that encourage both the students who take risks and the peers who support their classmates. The trick is to vary the rewards and times they are given so that the students do not catch on—this will help educators avoid creating artificial-praise environments that foster false confidence. Teachers must let students know they understand that trying new skills and learning new material can be intimidating, especially in a classroom full of peers. However, students also need to know that teachers will appreciate and support all efforts, whether they lead to failure or success. When a pupil is not successful, teachers should clearly indicate that they believe the student can do better—that the student can achieve better. Teachers not only need to encourage risk, but also assure students that confronting risk is safe in the classroom—and that they will be there to help them recover from missteps.

Finally, another critical piece for building authentic confidence is offering environments for students to take initiative. I spoke earlier about the Millennial Generation struggling with taking initiative at work because they were raised with sets of instructions on how to do things. This lack of initiative has birthed a fear of tackling ideas or problems. It has created a group of individuals who are hesitant to step forward. The good news is that corporate America is helping to rectify this, and we are seeing many Millennials start their own companies and take initiative. Regardless, this generation is experiencing a handicap, and our entire society is learning from that.

I met a student last summer who had recently graduated from

my school. He'd just written a book on the effects of big corporations utilizing data and how this will continue to have a profound effect on society. Currently, he is working on solving some big issues in education. He has been very successful thus far, and I've analyzed the key components of his success. He said that his teachers and parents encouraged him to always take the initiative to start something. He was pushed to take steps, no matter where they would lead. Sometimes, he said, it led him to failure, but failure was always a future recipe for success, because he learned from his mistakes. He knew his teachers would help and encourage him, no matter the size of the challenges—global warming, poverty, education, etc...and his resources taught him that if he didn't try, he wouldn't be able to succeed. Try he did, and succeed he has. He wrote a musical symphony piece in high school and even found time to volunteer—all because he learned that without initiative, nothing would change or improve. Did I mention he is still an undergraduate in college? Watch out, world! This young person is just one of many I've seen taking initiative to help others, create products, or stand up for their peers.

Initiative encourages belief in the possibility of opportunities; those who possess it see opportunities where others see obstacles and barriers. Students who proactively start projects and work diligently usually do better than those who procrastinate. While initiative is a personal trait, it can be encouraged and modeled. Learning to take initiative independently and consistently trying new things are authentic confidence builders. Teachers can build this behavior in students by allowing them to make decisions within the classroom. These can be as small as identifying ways to improve the lunch line, or as big as letting them decide the order of the daily classroom tasks. This promotes critical thinking, which definitely works in tandem with initiative.

Another powerful tool is teachers modeling initiative themselves. Teachers achieve daily in the classroom due to taking initiative. They should take the time to voice out loud to students that they are taking initiative, why they are doing it, and what the results are. A student who sees a teacher face, struggle with, and overcome problems also sees that taking initiative will help build his or her own inner-confidence.

Any classroom activity that builds initiative must contain rules, challenges, and complexities inherent to the real world. Students must face intellectual, interpersonal, and intrapersonal challenges that go beyond grades. A clear sign that initiative is not taking place in a classroom is the presence of boredom among students. Teachers must be cognizant of this, and counter it by creating initiative amongst students by displaying it themselves.

As previously stated, the classroom plays a pivotal role in developing authentic confidence in students. Our current mandates create roadblocks for teachers trying to instill this within each student. Classroom time is critical for conversations, providing feedback, and diving deeper into thoughts and questions. Building genuine confidence in children depends upon teachers supporting students' development of these skills. Not every student who graduates or moves up to another grade level will fully gain the authentic confidence needed to be successful in the workplace. However, knowing that these traits begin developing during the formative years allows for the creation and growth of a student's foundation.

We have always known that teachers play a crucial role in helping kids develop their confidence. We have to be realistic with our students about their skills and abilities and create paths for them to obtain the confidence to push forward. We cannot offer compliments in place of true, genuine growth. As Kay Hymowitz

(2009) wrote in the *Los Angeles Times*, "Telling kids how smart they are can be counterproductive. Many children who are convinced they are little geniuses tend not to put much effort in to their work. Others are troubled by the latent anxiety of adults who feel it necessary to praise them constantly" (p. 1). To develop authentic confidence in the classroom, there will have to be some tough conversations. Sometimes teachers may not have support from parents or be undermined by outside influences beyond their control. However, focusing on developing resilience and initiative while providing a challenging environment that encourages risk will give students the authentic confidence needed to face future challenges. Teachers have a tough job, and I admire them every day for what they do. Many say teaching is one of the hardest things they have ever done. The reward, for both educators and the world, is seeing students with the confidence to tackle challenges without fear, while knowing that every experience is a life lesson.

CHAPTER SIX

BUILDING CONFIDENCE OUTSIDE THE CLASSROOM

"You gain strength, courage, and confidence by every experience in which you really stop to look fear in the face. You are able to say to yourself, 'I lived through this horror. I can take the next thing that comes along.'"
—*Eleanor Roosevelt*

Building confidence in children can be so difficult because the multiple environments they interact in have profound effects on them. Teachers often remark that if the parents, coaches, and communities children interact with would just step away, then the teachers could achieve so much more. I usually then remark that such a statement is unrealistic and counterproductive to building authentic confidence. A child must build confidence in multiple environments to succeed in new, potentially uncomfortable future environments. If children only build authentic confidence in the academic setting, they garner only one piece of the puzzle. The experiences they can then recall and rely on for guidance are limited, as well as the cross-pollination of thought patterns which foster growth and direction in future decision-making paradigms.

Students gain authentic confidence not only in the classroom, but in the outside world via extracurricular activities and communities. I remember my parents always bringing my siblings and me to various community and social events. We were encouraged to talk to adults and engage in all types of conversations. As a child, I felt like I was able to be an adult early on and had a seat at the conversation table. Looking back, I'm sure my parents' friends were more enamored with the fact that we would engage in conversation, rather than the actual content we contributed to discussions. I often heard my parents' colleagues remark about how impressed they were with our abilities to uphold intellectual discourse at such young ages. I do not know if I was meant to hear these compliments or not, but it had a huge impact on my confidence in expressing opinions. The feedback was not just for the purpose of politely praising a friend's child. The feedback was genuine, and provided a foundation for me to build upon—a foundation for speaking up and letting my thoughts be heard. It gave me the confidence to talk in class on subjects that others veered away from. It also gave me the confidence in future jobs to present beneficial ideas and plans to upper management (instead of sitting back and waiting for directions).

One can see that the environment outside of the classroom has just as much, if not more, impact in supporting the foundation for building authentic confidence. In the following pages, I will examine three different areas where children experience and build confidence outside the classroom. I will look at the roles of instruments, sports, and service as pathways for growth. There are other pathways beside these for building confidence, but these areas are highly prevalent in most children's daily lives. Ensuring that the environments outside the classroom support what is happening inside the classroom—and vice versa—is imperative to building authentic confidence. As previously mentioned, when there is a disconnect between these environments, then false confidence and self-esteem levels develop and hinder coping with life's challenges.

TIME Magazine in 2014 reported that actively learning to play an instrument could help a child's confidence and academic achievement. Research has shown that learning to play a musical instrument is great for developing a strong mind. By actively playing music, youngsters' brains begin to hear and process sounds. By doing so, they develop "neurophysiological distinction" between certain sounds that can aid in literacy, self-esteem, and improved academic results (Kraus et al., 2014).

Nina Kraus, Jane Hornickel, Dana L. Strait, Jessica Slater, and Elaine Thompson of Northwestern University performed a study that looked at the success instrument-playing students experienced in college admissions and academics. They discovered a strong correlation between academic success and playing an instrument (Kraus et al., 2014). In fact, in analyzing the research coming from Northwestern's Auditory Neuroscience Laboratory, there seems to be a thread joining the articles about playing instruments and increased social and academic confidence. Authentic confidence is so inherent in musical education because children receive immediate feedback on their performances. Children can tell by the audience's response if they are playing well and also judge their skills by hearing themselves.

I mentioned several areas within the classroom that help build authentic confidence—a challenging environment, resilience, and risk. Playing an instrument involves all three of these. I have watched many children step up to the stage to perform for recitals. I enjoy seeing them next to or behind the stage before their turn. I especially like to watch the newer students who are giving their first recitals. You usually see them fidgeting and displaying clear discomfort. They pace and express anxious behavior in anticipation of performing in front of a crowd of (mostly) strangers. When they approach the stage, some take a deep breath, and others shake with fear. For those who make it all the way up on stage, they usually search the audience for that family member who offers a look of reassurance. The student begins to play, usually just as he or she had practiced the number many times before. When finished, they take their bows while the crowd applauses, and one can almost physically see the weight of self-doubt lifting and confidence rising from their feet up to their shoulders. It is amazing to see this transformation.

Why do they feel this way and why does it lead to building authentic confidence? The influence that performance experiences have on self-confidence depends on the perceived difficulty of the task, the effort expended, and the amount of guidance received; it is argued that performance accomplishments in difficult, independent, and early-in-life tasks carry great confidence value (Bandura, 1986). Learning and playing an instrument builds confidence through a social comparison process with others (Festinger, 1954). As students learn an instrument, they begin with less experience, and thus rely on others to judge their own capabilities. Building one's authentic confidence through monitoring and modeling other music students and audience feedback has been shown to enhance and increase confidence levels in terms of performance or personal characteristics (George et al., 1992; Gould and Weiss, 1981). When a student transforms from sounding like a foghorn to beautifully melodious, they benefit from a sense of accomplishment and pride due to the hard work and effort put into the achievement.

Milwaukee Youth Symphony Orchestra (MYSO) is a unique organization that works with students from all backgrounds and teaches them to play instruments. They have developed a community outreach program called Progressions. Progressions is an intensive string-training program providing private and orchestral instruction in violin, viola, cello, and bass to third and fourth grade Milwaukee students with little or no experience. One of the primary goals of Progressions is building increased participation in MYSO from students of minority populations that have been historically underrepresented in youth orchestra programs. The program provides instruments, free lessons, books, and transportation on a weekly basis for students who are interested in music and nominated by their principals. The students must commit to the program and maintain their academic grades. The program is designed to be rigorous, offers clear expectations of the students and their families, and helps improve musical performance alongside developmental and cognitive skills.

Most of the schools that MYSO works with are from the Milwaukee Public School District (MPS). MPS has had 55 of its 157 schools fail to meet expectations by state standards in the past. Mary Reinders (2015) with Reinders Research has been studying the effects of the MYSO Progressions program on this population for several years. MYSO and Mary have used pre- and post-evaluation tools from UW-Milwaukee and other professionals to measure the effects of various impacts on student academics and behavior. Teachers, parents, and MYSO instructors participated in the pre- and post-surveys. Results relayed that over 50% of students showed growth by seven points or more in areas such as self-esteem, leadership, teamwork, problem solving, problem identification, and self-expression (Reinders, 2015).

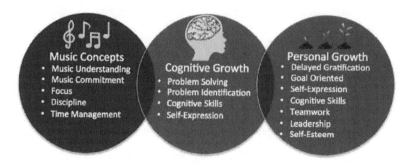

All of these are key components in building authentic confidence. Just as important as the growth in these areas was how outside activities positively impacted students' experiences inside the classroom. Authentic confidence cannot be solely built within the walls of the school—it must be leveraged in coordination with outside activities and organizations. What makes MYSO so successful is that it challenges the students, holds them accountable, and there is little sugarcoating regarding their abilities and work ethics while learning their instruments. MYSO also demonstrates that building authentic confidence does not pertain to a particular culture, as the program spans across ethnic, cultural, and economic boundaries. We can see the results firsthand in the attitudes and demeanors of the students, but even more so in the academic strides these students make. There are tangible results showing that when we build and support authentic confidence in students, doors open and progress is made. These outlets give students foundations to build upon, secure and assuring bases to launch from and fall back upon.

Sports are another way to build authentic confidence, but they can act as inhibitors, as well. My daughter and I recently watched an episode of Disney's *Girl Meets World* called "Girl Meets STEM." In the episode, the character Auggie Matthews returns home from a soccer game with a trophy. Auggie says to his mom, "Aren't you proud of me for getting this trophy? I had such a good attitude when the ball rolled by me into the goal." His mom reluctantly and sarcastically responds with support, even commenting that a mom from the other team thanked her for letting Auggie play (so her child looked better). They went on talking about the twenty-nine goals scored against them and how the score did not matter.

While I certainly believe in good sportsmanship and not taking winning too seriously, this type of unqualified praise simply for the sake of praise only establishes a sense of false confidence that provides little support later in life. In addition, it not only hurts the children who are falsely praised for efforts they did not deliver, but also diminishes the efforts of those children who worked really hard.

Later in the episode, a friend of Auggie's from the other team enters and realizes that Auggie got the same trophy she did. The little girl is furious for the exact reason just mentioned. She explains to Auggie that praise without effort is wrongly given. The episode continues with the girl teaching Auggie some soccer skills. In the end, Auggie starts to display authentic confidence because he built skills rather than just being told he was good to protect his feelings (Zwick, 2016).

Athletics are a great example of how we have falsely praised children and created a lack of authentic confidence with rippling effects in school and life. What's interesting is that even if you give every athlete a trophy, children still know who is better, tried the hardest, and receiving a trophy "just because." When children enter the workforce, would we expect them to be given business by everyone they interact with? If they were in sales, would we expect that everyone would buy their products? This is the mindset being instilled when every child gets a trophy for participation. We are conditioning them to be unable to cope with feelings of failure or rejection.

Professor Margaret Talbot, President of the International Council for Sport Science and Physical Education, once wrote that sports, dance, and other challenging physical activities are distinctively powerful ways of helping young people learn to 'be themselves' and build their self-confidence. She suggested that physical activities teach children to question detractors, and come to view themselves and their potential in a more confident manner (Bailey, 2014.)

Mina Samuels's *Run Like a Girl: How Strong Women Make Happy Lives* offers perspectives of girls and women whose lives have been transformed by sports. Samuels speaks from personal experience:

> Over the years that followed my "discovery" of running, my self-confidence grew, and feeding off the accomplishments I achieved in sports—setting new personal bests, winning a little local race, surviving the setbacks of injuries and marathons gone wrong—I discovered a capacity within myself that I never knew I had. I wasn't just physically stronger than I expected, I thought of myself as a different person, as someone with more potential, broader horizons, bigger possibilities. I saw that I could push myself and take risks, not just in sports, but elsewhere, too. The competition in sports, as in life, was not with someone else, it was with myself. To "compete" was to discover my own potential to do better, to hold my own self to a higher standard, to expect more of myself—and deliver (Samuels, 2011, p. 12).

Samuels clearly illustrates authentic confidence as a base or foundation that her success and drive stem from. There is a widely held belief among parents that the development of competence or expertise in sporting skills can help a child learn a greater sense of personal value. Researchers have found that physical activities play a powerful role in strengthening physical self-worth and self-esteem. While the relationship is complex, a positive perception of physical self-worth seems to be an important factor in general positive self-perceptions, especially during childhood and early adolescence. There is a risk of superiority complexes developing, but providing and establishing a healthy, grounded, realistic view of abilities and efforts in sports help build the authentic confidence needed to be successful later in life.

As a parent, there is perhaps nothing more frustrating than seeing a child presented with a great opportunity...and then become paralyzed with fear and uncertainty. We want children to develop autonomy and intrinsic motivation to set the bar high in life—while having the foundational confidence to continue chasing dreams, even if obstacles are placed in the way. Sports are a great way to teach some of those valuable lessons, if done correctly. However, when we protect our children from failure in sports, academics, or life by removing obstacles or lessening the challenge, we prevent them from developing the authentic confidence and determination to chase their dreams and goals.

There is a great story written about Hall of Fame quarterback Steve Young. He talks about his father, Grit. Grit taught him authentic confidence by saying, "If you work hard, you can do it. When faced with challenges, work harder and overcome those challenges" (Doman, 2014, p. 2). His father insisted that failure was but a bump in the road to success—and it was up to the individual to overcome that bump and keep going forward. To do so required confidence. Steve challenged that advice when he first started playing for BYU. Discouraged, homesick, and feeling like a "big tackling dummy for the defense," Steve called his dad and said, "I think I'd like to come home" (Doman, 2016, p. 3).

Grit's reply was, "Okay, Steve, you can quit. But you can't come home!" (Doman, 2016, p. 3). With nowhere else to go, Steve took the tough road and stayed at BYU, therefore overcoming the bump in the road all the way to the NFL Hall of Fame. Steve broke record after record in what turned out to be a phenomenal football career. Steve says, "When things are hard and you're young, a lot of times you're looking for exit doors," and, "There are no exits unless you open them up" (Doman, 2014, p. 4). Steve mentions that you have to have the confidence to open those doors and have faith in your direction. Due to his father's influence, instead of escaping, Steve's focus became figuring out how he could build his authentic confidence. "The best thing my dad can do is to put me in a situation to have a chance to find out how good I can get, and give me that stuff to find out, because otherwise you exit stage left along the way and you never find out," Steve said (Doman, 2014, p. 4).

This is why sports can and should be included in the confidence toolbox. Building authentic confidence, as I've said, does not happen overnight. But if we artificially prop up our children with false praise and senses of accomplishment, we are whittling away at their abilities to face challenges and bumps in the road.

Much like sports and playing instruments, learning to give back to the community provides huge opportunities for confidence. Research indicates that individuals stuck in the cycle of low self-esteem show a tendency toward excessive self-focus. A recent study showed that the best way to boost self-esteem was to think about others. According to University of Michigan psychologists Jennifer Crocker and Amy Canevello (2011), "Nothing makes you more proud of yourself than knowing that you are making a positive difference in the lives of other people" (p. 1010).

Knowing one can make a difference builds authentic confidence within the self. When we serve others and create a positive experience for someone other than ourselves, we build authentic confidence in realizing our ability to affect change. We can then turn back to these experiences when challenged in other areas of life. By sharing our talents and time, we are confirming that we have something worthwhile to contribute, we can make a difference, and our presence is appreciated. Children feel that as much as adults do. This is partly why we see so many children willing and independently offering to help others. Whether starting a food drive or reading books to other children, these build confidence as they discover they have something to offer this world.

My daughter came home from school one day when she was in first grade. She had beautiful honey brown hair (and still does). People would regularly comment on its shine. My wife had worked hard to help her brush and wash it to remove dirt and dust from days of fun-filled outdoor adventures. My wife even remarked at times that she wished she had our daughter's hair.

That specific day, our daughter came home and announced that she wanted to cut her hair off. I think my wife and I shouted, "No!" in unison, as we could not imagine why she would want to do such a thing. When we asked her why, she said she had learned about Locks of Love. In her first grade vocabulary, she told us Locks of Love was a charitable organization that provided hair to financially disadvantaged children suffering from long-term medical hair loss due to cancer or other illnesses. She said that her donated hair would create hair pieces and prosthetics for girls her age, and she wanted to share. She wanted them to feel better because being ill is not fun. She thought that donating her hair would help to restore their confidence and attitude, enabling them to face the world and their peers.

To say the least, my wife and I were beaming with pride, but also still very concerned. How would my daughter feel walking into class the next day with a fraction of the flowing hair she'd had the day before? My wife and I wondered how she would respond to no longer receiving compliments on her hair. What would she do if kids pointed out her hair and made her feel uncomfortable? My wife and I talked with her (in a "first grade way") and described some of the challenges the haircut would present. Well, my daughter is very determined, and she had made up her mind that she wanted to donate her hair. And she did.

That might have been the first time I realized authentic confidence growth can happen in children when they offer to help others. It was not necessarily the act of giving her hair, but the pride she gained from doing so. She marched into class the next day to gasps of, "What did you do?" My daughter proudly and confidently told everyone why she did it, which inspired others to follow. It built authentic confidence in her because she could lead and be an inspiration to others.

As an educator, I see this happen time and time again. Children thrive on being able to give back. But, I always warn parents against forcing the act of giving or donating time. It can have the opposite effect. Don't get me wrong, I think suggesting volunteering to our students helps them beneficially understand and experience civic responsibility. What I am referring to is dictating when, where, and how much. When students choose where and how to give, it creates a stronger, more independent authentic confidence. If we order them to volunteer, we produce a negative effect. Some studies show that forcing students to volunteer creates civic awareness and can lead to an increase in voting. Although voting is very important, the longer-standing personal impact should be the positive feedback and confidence building associated with long-term volunteering. For many children, opportunities to volunteer allow them to interact in an environment that may be outside of their comfort zones. Areas such as homeless shelters, veteran's homes, or hospitals with cancer patients would more than likely make children (as well as adults) experience discomfort. To volunteer in such an environment and gain comfort would build authentic confidence. Overcoming fears or preconceived notions would, in turn, build a healthy foundation for future interactions.

Volunteering is a huge step for children toward learning that they can tackle social issues, community challenges, and even health issues. It builds authentic confidence as much as other extracurricular activities they may be involved in.

Whether it be in art, music, sports, volunteering, or many other activities, children build authentic confidence outside the classroom just as much as much as they do inside it. The compounding effects a child experiences by focusing on building authentic confidence in multiple ways can have profound results later in life. School subjects and extracurricular activities complement each other and develop a well-rounded, socially skilled, and confident student. We know that being involved in extracurricular activities increases confidence, motivation, and better time-management.

Children build authentic confidence when they are able to build skills through different experiences in an organic way, free from the pressure of parents and the outside world. Parents play an enormous role in a child's ability to develop authentic confidence outside of the classroom. Children naturally look to their parents for guidance, comfort, reassurance, and learning how to behave and believe in this world. How parents handle challenges and possible failures can have the biggest influence on children, and this influence is even stronger because they control their children's involvement in extracurricular activities. Children must acquire skills that are supported by parents and teachers; this will construct a foundation for them that can withstand challenges and harbor perseverance. Children need to positively perceive their own skills, qualifications, and performances and know that deep down, they can overcome obstacles and push forward.

I had the privilege of watching my son take karate lessons and perform more advanced moves quickly. His end-of-the-year skill evaluation earned him a higher belt, and it increased his confidence in those skills and himself as a whole. He gained authentic confidence with which to go for more challenging belts in karate. If we build authentic confidence in our children's lives, both inside and outside the classroom, we prepare them for the challenges of tomorrow. We know this, yet we seem to continually find ways to dismantle students' abilities to do so. We harbor fear that children will not be confident in life, so we overprotect— which impairs their chances to build genuine confidence, or provides false confidence. Children have a natural inclination to discover their own interests and developmental activities outside the classroom. Parents, teachers, and friends should foster these proclivities by encouraging them to independently further their skill development, while concretely and realistically acknowledging children's accomplishments.

Children who engage in extracurricular activities outside the classroom have better opportunities to develop authentic confidence through supportive, healthily stimulating, and challenging situations. These are part of the growing list of items in an authentically confident child's toolbox.

CHAPTER SEVEN

WHAT CONFIDENCE LOOKS LIKE IN THE WORLD

"Be confident enough to encourage confidence in others."
—*Ron Kaufman*

So we've discussed what building authentic confidence entails in the classroom and how extracurricular activities play a significant role. But why does all this matter? I have presented research illustrating that a lack of confidence can have a profound effect on learning and a longitudinal effect on lives. Educators are constantly employing the Wiggins and McTighe (1998) Understanding by Design method to design a path and plan for achieving goals. Wiggins and McTighe (1998) explain that "many teachers begin with textbooks, favored lessons, and time-honored activities rather than deriving those tools from targeted goals or standards. We are advocating the reverse: One starts with the end—the desired results (goals or standards)—and then derives the curriculum from the evidence of learning (performances) called for by the standard and the teaching needed to equip students to perform" (p. 15). Educators tell students and parents that they need an idea of where they want to go in order to get there. However, teachers themselves seldom think about or consider where a child may be twenty or thirty years in the future. They may feel there are too many variables and unknowns. I disagree.

I often hear, "We are teaching children of tomorrow for careers that have yet to be envisioned." While I certainly agree that we do not know what jobs may exist in the future, I think if we look to history, we can recognize the skills necessary to bring those far-fetched career ideas to fruition. I'll use taking a trip as an analogy to illustrate what I mean.

Let's start at home. As we prepare for the flight, we start making a list of things we need. We think about the suitcase and clothes. We consider our destination's weather—heavy coat or flip-flops? We think about the currency and money necessary to enjoy food, drinks, and souvenirs. We also might consult a book or app about the destination covering its culture and language. We might need some communication lessons, a passport, and obviously, cell phones and computers.

We get to the airport and prepare to board the plane. However, when we arrive, there are no signs telling us where the planes are going. We are told to board a plane, and the destination will be revealed upon arrival. Seeing as though the destination is now unknown, is there anything we would have done differently when packing for the trip? Would we have prepared differently? How does one prepare for a completely unknown location?

Teachers experience exactly this when preparing students for life beyond school. Because they do not know each child's destination, they tend to stop looking forward and think short-term. They simply get children to the airport, rather than equipping them for any kind of destination.

In order to prepare students for the challenges of life, we have to develop in them different sets of skills, resilience, and thought processes that enable them to thrive in new environments. Thriving requires an authentic confidence toolbox; children must see the world through a lens of opportunity, not a lens of fear. This should direct our teachers toward looking at the skills needed to succeed now *and* in the future. I'm not implying that teachers never think about what kids need for an unknown tomorrow...but I am implying that we need to put greater focus on these skills and their development because they are consistently needed, no matter how the world changes.

Authentic confidence is one of those skills. Yet, as a society, we have chosen to ignore it. Whether it be lawnmower parents (those who remove any obstacles for children), helicopter parents (those who watch every move), or the need to make sure that children only see and feel happiness, we as a society have eroded authentic confidence. So what does authentic confidence look like beyond childhood? How do we guide parents, teachers, and society so that they can model it inside and outside the classroom?

Authentic confidence can be seen in many aspects and different stages of life. I am sure if we look around our schools, workplaces, and communities, we will observe authentic confidence in action. We see it most often in leaders. We know that in the classroom it presents itself in personal responsibility, hard work, resilience, the ability to extend oneself, etc. So what does it look like on a college campus, workplace, and in our community?

First, let's take a look at college campuses. College is the first step beyond the formative educational years. I believe it is the first real evidence that authentic confidence was being built as during youth. As a school administrator, I talk to many college admissions deans and professors about what skills they wish incoming students possessed. I hear about students' writing and argument construction, which, according to many, continues to dwindle in the incoming student populations. I also hear about students lacking personal responsibility.

One dean of admissions from a highly ranked university told me that his professors' biggest complaint was that students did not know how to use alarm clocks. I asked him what the alarm clock was an analogy for. He looked at me blankly, and then repeated, "Real alarm clocks." He said highly successful students usually had parents telling them when to get out of bed...and once mom and dad were gone, they didn't know what to do.

I would suggest that students who succeed in higher education are the ones who have built authentic confidence—and this is the source of their drive and responsibility. They are not afraid of failure and structure themselves to actively face it. A dean at Auburn University commented, "Those with true self-confidence are more successful. They may still make errors that result in problems, but they are not delayed by concerns about being defined by failure. The truly self-confident do not experience paralysis by analysis. The self-confident understand that some decisions must be made before all of the data is available. They calculate all that they can and then move forward with the most rational plan." Students with authentic confidence are able to move forward and are not afraid of failure. The same dean also said, "Confidence that one can fail (without self-deception), get up, try again, and then succeed is insurmountable as a determinant in being successful in life. I have the privilege of working with many young people as an Associate Dean for Academic Affairs in a professional school. Many young people that I work with are desperately scared that they might fail. They possess no confidence that they can fail, survive, try again and succeed. They have received many soccer trophies but no one ever trusted them enough to allow them the valuable life experience of failing." Successful students in higher education are those with the confidence to step forward and be different. Authentic confidence can been seen on campuses in those students who are seeking opportunities, unlike others who shy away from them for fear of failure or success.

I remember talking to an alumnus of my current school (where I am an administrator) who attended Harvard. I asked him about his confidence. He was perplexed by my question, but went on to explain that he had come from a midsized Midwestern high school, was highly intelligent, and placed in what is considered one of the most intellectual and driven universities in the world. The personal consequences of failure at a school like Harvard is no joke. However, he felt that his authentic confidence was decently developed and would aid him. He told a story about taking the freshman science placement exam in his first days there. He did well enough to skip his freshman science course, but his advisor highly opposed this. He explained to the advisor that with his authentic confidence—and his knowing that if he worked hard and used resources—he could move on up to sophomore-level science. He did so, he worked harder than ever before—and succeeded. Having just graduated from Harvard a year ago, he already owns his own successful startup company and is looking forward to his next adventure.

Possessing authentic confidence offers our children the ability to seek out opportunities, move forward when others stand still, and view failure as just a bump on the path to the destination. A good friend of mine at the University of Kentucky at Lexington said that self-confidence "definitely seems to be related to success as a faculty member and university student. Those with confidence are more likely to strive for high levels of accomplishment and to push back when directed in a way that may not make sense or be appropriate."

Research shows that through the college experience, students improve self-confidence and enhance their social wealth while embracing the personal identity of a 'learner' (Burns & Sinfield, 2003). Professors often know exactly which students have authentic confidence and those who don't. Those who lack authentic confidence are seen feeling defeated from time to time. These students often comment on who seems smarter or better than they are. They often chastise and compare themselves to others excessively. Stanford University assures students that individuals with genuine confidence don't judge others and are not self-absorbed; these people see great value in helping others achieve and see their potentials, as well (Standford, 2016).

Students with authentic confidence take full advantage of higher educational environments because they fully understand the opportunities available to them if they apply themselves, push beyond their comforts zones, and work hard. It's seen in labs, the dining hall, and even in athletics. With over 55% of undergraduates dropping out of college, one can only speculate that most students are not prepared to face the challenges of higher education (Weissmann, 2014). They do not have the confidence to believe in themselves. However, those that do have a greater success rate in achieving degrees. The National Center for Education Statistic (NCES) (2014) recently released a longitudinal study in which only 31% of 2002 sophomores graduated with a bachelor's degree by 2012. 57% of sophomores in private schools graduated by 2012. The trend seems to be that private schools with smaller classes and more time for building relationships and character have students with higher confidence levels. UCLA's Higher Education Research Institute has research documenting such, especially with girls who attended single-sex private schools (Wyer, 2009). Not to say that students from public schools do not develop authentic confidence, but the percentage of college graduates from private schools certainly points to their educational structure as one that promotes authentic confidence.

Authentic confidence is certainly observable, and a necessary component of fully engaging the opportunities on college and university campuses. Research has shown that students who succeed in higher education have greater chances of being successful in their future careers and lives.

With that in mind, what does authentic confidence look like after college and university experiences? How does authentic confidence propel one to greater opportunities beyond formative education? Experience has taught me that, for many, authentic confidence becomes harder to develop once they enter the workforce. That does not mean it cannot be developed then, but once one is working, there are additional roadblocks that impede ability. Negative "can't-do" attitudes developed in childhood are usually cemented and difficult to remove in adulthood. Without the foundation of authentic confidence, we do not have the tools to overcome negativity or challenges. Adults tend to get stuck.

Let me give you an example of the opposite. Look back in your history at your friends or colleagues. Now think of a time when you said to yourself, "Wow, I wish I could that." Your friend or colleague more than likely had a foundation of authentic confidence. We see it all the time when we observe people who make career changes, move to a new area or country, and even when we see people tackle disease and obesity. This is a dynamic world we work in, and we are constantly challenged to manage changing situations and conflict. We have obstacles to overcome and opportunities to take advantage of. Authentic confidence can help. People with authentic confidence are able to show that they can handle any situation and maintain a positive outlook. This is not always an easy feat, but no matter how stressed one feels inside, maintaining a good posture and positive outlook takes mental strength (and the will to say, "I can and will prosper"). Authentic confidence makes working outside of comfort zones possible, and makes it much easier to become accustomed to work habits and workday management.

When change happens in any organization, other individuals will follow a person with confidence because they'll be looking for direction and someone with a positive and confident manner. Authentic confidence enables an individual to encourage others to adapt to evolving situations in the work environment. Remaining positive and confident can be the key to standing out from the crowd, which leads to advancement within an organization. Authentic confidence is contagious and those who have it inspire others to harness and use it, too.

Let me give you an example of what I mean. I recently moved to Milwaukee, Wisconsin, to become the Head of School for a K-12 private school. One of my goals was to design a path for this school to effectively transfer the establishment's knowledge and culture to new employees and future administrators. In business terms, this is called "succession planning." As I usually do when I land in a new environment, I quickly find key leaders in the community who seem to have intrinsic, everyday authentic confidence. It's not hard to find them, because upon calling them, those with authentic confidence are happy to help and open up their networks of people. One of these connections introduced me to the Global Chief Marketing Officer at GE Healthcare in Milwaukee. That individual introduced me to Bob Cancalosi, Director of Global Customer Leadership for GE Crotonville, who had dealt with succession planning and management in the past. If you are unaware of the human resource department at GE, let me fill you in: GE recruits the brightest minds it can find and relentlessly cultivates its leaders, training them at its legendary in-house management school called Crotonville, located in Ossining, NY, about 45 minutes north of Manhattan. In addition to world-class CEOs like Jeff Immelt and his predecessor, Jack Welch, the GE system has produced numerous successful executives like Jim McNerny of Boeing, Chrysler's Bob Nardelli, and Dave Calhoun of the Nielsen Co. Many of today's top companies learn their management training techniques from GE. Bob Cancalosi was based out of Crotonville, but lived in Milwaukee.

I did not know until my first meeting with him that he had been with GE for over 30 years. To say the least, Bob had some knowledge to share with me. Our first meeting was incredible. As our conversation began, we talked about a management technique he'd developed at GE that utilized journaling. Not just any type of journaling, but journaling for mapping ideas and conversations to leverage thoughts. It is an incredible tool that every manager should use. His insight was inspiring. I could see that he had authentic confidence by his ability to help leaders become more successful than they imagined.

One day, as we sat working on a future journaling project in a restaurant in Milwaukee, I asked him why he was helping me. He looked perplexed. I explained that here was a GE Crotonville Leadership Development Executive who speaks with CEOs around the world, guest lectures at most of the top ten business schools in the world, and probably has a mile-long project list on his desk... Why would he be helping some administrator from a local private school? His answer almost knocked me out of my seat.

Bob said that he had all this authentic confidence in his ability to lead executives and managers in impacting ways. However, it was not until I'd given him a dose of confidence regarding how powerful his journaling techniques were that he could take the next step and write his book on the subject. As opposed to magnets that repel, there was a completely opposite reaction where authentic confidence attracted authentic confidence and the forces of two individuals generated a relationship where one plus one equaled three.

This story illustrates how authentic confidence is contagious and those who have it inspire others to use their own strengths. We see it every day, and it adds to the saying, "Success attracts success." Authentically confident individuals are always sharing ideas and helping others, as they understand that everything we do is a learning moment, whether it be a failure or success. Authentically confident adults face challenges and obstacles with drive and ambition. We admire those who take the risks we feel we personally cannot. This does not mean we do not have authentic confidence other places in life, but many lack confidence in their work. For adults, fear is the ultimate authentic confidence killer—whether it be fear of success, moving, being alone, or something else. Fear, in my opinion, is just discomfort with the unknown. But by building authentic confidence, we face that unknown by challenging it, and not letting fear hold us captive.

So how does one build authentic confidence after completing a degree? As we gain authentic confidence and use it in positive ways, it becomes a powerful tool for advancing closer to our personal and professional goals. However, people can easily shift from authentic confidence to over-confidence, which can lead to an uncontrolled ego. I have learned firsthand that managers and leaders with authentic confidence need to focus on sustaining and enhancing their own confidence and also eliciting it in those they lead. When it comes to developing authentic confidence as adults, we should follow many of methods mentioned for the classroom and outside the classroom. Confident adults are underrepresented in many industries, government positions, and board rooms. This is why we are continually looking for leaders. Building authentic confidence is one step toward getting off that sticky floor and moving up the corporate ladder.

Here are my suggestions for those adults looking to build their authentic confidence. I try and use these in my career, as well.

First, we should be aware of our word choices. We do not want to undermine our confidence by using phrases like, "I can't," or, "I failed." We must use confident words in full, strong statements, not gentle suggestions, when speaking with coworkers or the community.

Second, we must believe that we are confident. If we have can-do attitudes, they take us a long way. I remember when I was first asked to be a Head of School. I had no mentor to guide me, but I knew if I believed in myself and worked hard to learn from every possible opportunity, I could succeed. How we walk, shake hands, and make (or avoid) eye contact tells others whether or not we have authentic confidence. If we "walk the walk," we will feel more confident and have a more positive outlook on ourselves and our organizations.

Third, people want to hear our opinions in constructive and helpful manners. I always encourage both students and adults to speak up and express their ideas. Don't over-assert yourself, but find the balance between holding back what you're thinking and dominating the conversation.

Fourth: do not to let fear get in the way. If everyone is going in one direction and you feel the other way is the better route, then go the other direction. It may be what works and it may not. If not, then you learned something, and that is just as powerful.

I remember when I was working for a private equity firm that owned private schools worldwide. I was a headmaster at one of their schools in Florida. Each month, we had an operations meeting with the executive leadership group in Chicago via video conferencing. Our CEO always told the headmasters that this was our meeting, although it often felt like the Spanish Inquisition. (It wasn't *that* bad, but you get the point.) One meeting, I decided to go for it. I decided to risk being too forward and used the CEO's own suggestion to lead the executives in the meeting. We had a big project going on, and I was waiting on information from the executives in marketing, finance, development, and administration. I thought, *I have them all in the room together...why not direct the conversation?* I went over my operations report, as was normal, and answered a few questions. Also, as per usual, the CEO asked if there was anything else needing discussing, and most headmasters were eager to finish the meeting and close down the video conferencing. I decided that was my opportunity, and I went from executive to executive, in a polite manner, letting them know what I needed from them and when in order to keep the project moving. They were all caught by surprise, but I won the praise of the CEO. He actually started laughing halfway through my requests and questions, expressing how much he loved that I was holding them accountable. It was a huge boost to my authentic confidence and taught me some very valuable lessons.

Building authentic confidence often requires going a different direction or taking some risks that others may not. Too often I see people without the genuine confidence to pick up and advance themselves, whether in a career, moving to another city, or a part of their personal lives. They tend to complain about their current situations, yet do nothing to overcome the misery they are in. I am a big believer in taking control of your own future. We must realize that we develop authentic confidence if we go in our own directions, wherever they may lead.

Finally, I believe that most people fail to leverage their

feedback from mangers or customers to build authentic confidence. When it's time to sit down with the boss and assess our performances, we mustn't be shy. We should be armed with a list of accomplishments (as well as goals) for the coming year. Bosses appreciate forthrightness. But we have to listen carefully to feedback. Managers and leaders with strong confidence will help us grow ours. They will give us honest feedback. Be careful, though—if they feel that we do not care or will not listen, they will know that and question it. Authentic confidence doesn't come naturally for us, but it remains an important component for advancing in the professional world.

The bottom line is that no one is stopping us from building confidence after higher education. I say the same thing to students all the time. If you want to write a book, write a book. If you want to build a business, build it. You just have to believe in yourself and remove the barriers that have hindered you in the past. By removing those barriers, we build authentic confidence. Being successful in our careers means that we embrace our authentic confidence, and will let it help us reach the top. We will need to work hard. Additionally, we will need help from others who have built their authentic confidence. In fact, these two aspects are equally important.

Authentic confidence means believing in what we do and how we do it. People who lack authentic confidence tend to feel that the outside world 'controls' them, while those with authentic confidence don't let outside conflicts or obstacles stand in the way. We shouldn't fear stepping out of our comfort zones and reaching for the stars. We all can improve upon and benefit from having authentic confidence within ourselves, at work, and in social situations. The hope for the future is that students can begin developing it in school so they have foundations to build upon. It is very easy for people without authentic confidence to get stuck and feel trapped. Those who challenge themselves and face the hard work needed to overcome those obstacles achieve authentic confidence to move forward. A funny thing happens when one has a strong base of authentic confidence: the required hard work gets easier...not any smaller in size, but easier, because one has the ability to persevere through. Each of us has the ability to grow authentic confidence and thrive, wherever we may be in our lives.

CHAPTER EIGHT

CONCLUSION

There is a saying, "There is no elevator in life." There are only stairs when seeking our goals or success. Very few of us wake up one day to find our goals magically achieved. Rather, hard work compounded over many years enables us to achieve these goals. How do we teach our kids that this is the reality of the world? How do we teach our students that there are young people out there who have the same goals, but are willing to put in more effort? There are those who are willing to set aside distractors and focus on the hard work needed to succeed.

When parents provide too much elevation during early childhood and young adult development, they handicap children in understanding the process, hard work, and steps needed to achieve true success. These steps and hard work are what build authentic confidence in a person. One cannot have authentic confidence in everything, but the idea is to build it specifically in areas that help us achieve our goals. Those successful professionally and in life often say that they have been learning since the day they were born and will continue doing so until the day they die. However, the ability to develop authentic confidence in several areas sets the stage for taking on challenges, not fearing hard work, and facing the unknown. There was an article on CNN.com about students who got into Ivy League schools this year. This article featured Kelly Hyles, who lived in Queens. Kelly moved to the United States from Guyana when she was eleven years old. She expressed how her mother was a hard worker. Her mom worked two jobs to support their family. (Pause: this is the first example of how Kelly started building her authentic confidence.) One can gain authentic confidence by having a good role model. Her mother showed her what hard work looked like and why it was important. It gave her the foundational belief that if she worked really hard, she could achieve great things. Thus, she gained a platform of confidence to accomplish her own goals.

Back to the story: Kelly now attends a specialized school in Harlem, New York, for math, science, and engineering. She commutes over an hour and a half to school each day. She is also one of less than two-dozen African American students in her senior class of more than 130. This student ratio is low, and Kelly found it troubling. She said, "I am convinced that the decrease is not due to intellectual aptitude, but to lack of preparation and confidence" (O'Brian, 2016, p. 2).

I have found in my career that students with a base of authentic confidence seek and apply themselves to problems that they deem important. They are not afraid to tackle issues, and usually take some sort of personal responsibility in solving problems. Kelly did exactly this when she partnered with the DREAM program, which helps prepare students for the admissions and entry tests for these specialized high schools. "I cannot see my race or gender as limiting factor, but rather as a reason to work harder," she said (O'Brian, 2016, p. 3). Her efforts should be commended, but they did not build her authentic confidence. Her authentic confidence came from seeing that she could face a challenge and make a difference for herself and others. Her authentic confidence was certainly built by working hard and sacrificing, but it was also aided by a good role model and her seeing experiences as opportunities to learn and grow. These experiences made her highly adaptable and able to fit in anywhere.

You see, authentic confidence happens when we combine guidance and support for children, rather than enabling and overprotecting. Authentic confidence gives our children the inertia to take on projects or hurdles, and doesn't impede them for the sake of protecting their pride and personalities. In trying to protect ourselves from perceived failure, we tend to avoid situations instead of striving for something better. Authentic confidence allows us to focus on the upside rather than the downside, no matter how significant the downside may be.

Individuals with a lack of authentic confidence are more concerned about how they will look if they fail and are overly focused on the "danger" of failure. If you criticize someone with low confidence, even just a little, they usually viciously defend themselves. They fear the house of cards falling down rather than seeing a new learning experience. Or they may find out they need to work harder than expected to achieve what they thought they already accomplished. We see this when looking at trophy kids who are commended for just participating. If you question a child from this kind of environment, they will defend why they got the trophy, even though they may not have worked to master the skills they received the trophy for. We see the consequences of such conditioning when people enter the workforce looking for praise just because they showed up to work on time.

Some have claimed that we are raising generations of deluded narcissists (Ablow, 2016). I would not go that far, but I do think that most people believe that adults who exhibit overprotective parenting behaviors are responsible for raising children who are more self-involved and lacking initiative. As the path to success is more crowded than ever, parents are trying to carve a channel through the congestion that will make it easier for their children to succeed. However, this only props children up on a shaky foundation that leaves them unsteady when they're set free into the real world. The shock of adulthood then hits them, unprepared, with simple things like realizing they may have to work weekends, understand the differences between 401(k) plans, and pay bills.

Duties and responsibilities in life and on the job are demanding and can present challenges. Each of the decisions we make derives real-world consequences. Children need to be equipped to think through scenarios and situations that will inevitably arise, not just for the sake of success, but also for the sake of being able to tackle problems and fears for a healthy self-understanding.

Up to this point, education has been simply pragmatic; teachers test students on specific content, so their pupils learn and memorize this specific content for just one test. Educators are challenged to push adolescents to understand hard work, resilience, and determination. Too often, students are not taught how to think through failures to find solutions—as with mathematics, where formulas are memorized and the numbers plugged in without an explanation as to what the real-world applications are.

Learning about the process of overcoming barriers is a good place to start. There is a modern trend toward equality and egalitarianism in academia and competitive school sports. We are now seeing the result of not having taught students to properly deal with failure. In fact, I would say failure is being outright avoided. It is becoming an increasingly common practice in academia and sports to preserve each student's sense of forged confidence, and as a result, students are not being told that their schoolwork is substandard and worthy of a failing grade. They are unable to build that authentic confidence needed for a strong approach to life. Students tell me that one of the main reasons they quit sports is because they are afraid to make mistakes and get criticized, yelled at, and benched. We know from years of researching professional athletes that great players bloom in environments where they do not fear mistakes, are encouraged to try and fail, and are taught that failure is a necessary part of the development process (Martin, 2015). Teachers, coaches, and parents who second-guess children's decisions and chastise them for trying their best and failing are creating a culture of fear that drives students to preserve their sense of safety through mediocrity.

We need to embrace failure and risk-taking in our children. Instead of just praising the result of a successful action, we need to start praising what students do immediately following a mistake to encourage coping, fortitude, and determination to work harder. We need to recognize that no such setting exists in general society that is sympathetic and concerned with an individual's self-esteem. In the real world, deficient work results in consequences. Learning from failure teaches resilience, grit, character, and makes one tougher and more capable of navigating life's inevitable ups and downs. It builds one's authentic confidence.

The story of Milton Hershey is a pertinent one in regard to authentic confidence. Hershey was born on September 13th, 1857, in Derry Township, Pennsylvania (Hershey, 2016). His parents separated when he was young, and his father was not around to help foster his growth. Hershey's upbringing was left to his mother, and this strict disciplinarian instilled in her son an appreciation for hard work. At the age of fourteen, Hershey, who'd dropped out of school the year before, expressed an interest in making candy and soon began working for a confectioner in Lancaster, Pennsylvania, with the help of his mother. Four years later, Hershey borrowed $150 from his aunt and set up his own candy shop in the heart of Philadelphia. For five years, Hershey poured all he had into the business, working hard toward success. However, that success did not come easily. Hershey closed shop and headed west, reuniting with his father in Denver, where he found work with another confectioner. It was there that he discovered caramel. It was soon after that Hershey wanted to try things on his own again and started businesses, first in Chicago, and later New York City. In both cases, Hershey again failed.

In 1883, he returned to Lancaster and, still convinced he could build a successful candy company, started the Lancaster Caramel Company. Within a few short years, Hershey had a thriving business and was shipping his caramels all over the country. He added chocolate, built a community around the factory, and even funded a school for orphans. His success illustrates why we're talking about building authentic confidence in children. His mother taught him to work hard and overcome obstacles. She taught him to be frugal and honorable in his dealings with others. Hershey learned from this, and we should learn from Hershey that failures should be treated as steppingstones to success. We should teach students to appreciate difficult lessons that will take them to the next level.

In a small town in Puerto Rico, a similar story demonstrated the importance of challenging children, some 111 years later. In 1994, Carlos Correa was born. From an early age, Carlos was taught to overcome. His story is similar to many in that he credits the people early in his life with helping him become the Major League Baseball (MLB) star he is today. He often talks about his coaches, and especially his dad, who played a very influential role in developing his foundation. "I had to grow up faster than most kids," Correa said. "I feel like the way I was raised and the work I did on my way here is making me feel more comfortable at this level" (Castrovince, 2015, p. 2).

Correa had to work with his father before and after school. It wasn't until late in the evenings and after dinner when they would go practice hitting and fielding baseballs. Correa remarks that his father taught him that if he wanted to practice, he had to get his other responsibilities finished first. He also taught him that if he wanted to be in MLB one day, he had to work hard, even when his friends were going to sleep or playing video games. His father, who worked as many as three jobs a day to pay for Carlos Jr.'s schooling, would have him lend a hand by fetching tools or helping around construction sites. On weekends, he'd make Carlos Jr. wash the family's cars. Some may consider this taxing on a child, but for Carlos Jr., it instilled both work ethic and a dream. Correa remarks, "I don't know how to describe it, but when you work hard for something and have goals and want to accomplish it, you feel like you deserve it" (Castrovince, 2015, p. 3).

The stories of Milton Hershey and Carlos Correa are not so different. The two had major obstacles between them and their dreams. But the early lessons from teachers, coaches, and parents enabled them to see that by taking the stairs, they could build a foundation of determination, resilience, and success through failure. They built their authentic confidence.

The road to building authentic confidence begins at an early age. The foundation certainly does not happen overnight; it evolves over time. It requires steps forward and steps back. It is up to teachers, parents, mentors, coaches, and communities to realize their effects on the formation of children's authentic confidence. We need to build the abilities of students and young adults so they can react and learn in a productive manner from challenges and failures. We see the struggles of people who did not develop those abilities and are now struggling to find it. We see that as we become more aware of the skills necessary to survive an increasingly changing world, finding ways over, underneath, and around obstacles is essential to achieving goals.

Students and young adults deserve to be challenged. We cannot simply continue being their wings and then expect them to soar like eagles when we toss them from the nest. Parents have an innate urge to protect their children and create better paths for them than the ones they traveled as children. However, we fail them when we don't prepare them for overcoming the obstacles in their lives. Building their authentic confidence gives them a toolbox with utensils to carve and create a future they can be proud of. Authentic confidence begins in the classroom, on the playing field, and at home—and it starts at an early age. It blooms with hope and the understanding that to build passion and their extraordinary selves, they must have a foundation, base, and guiding principles that drive them forward against any headwind. My hope is that this book continues an imperative conversation that many have started before me. Authentic confidence is just one piece of the puzzle—a very important piece, but one piece, nonetheless.

Children deserve this world's very best. But *our* very best must prepare them for life, its challenges, its obstacles, and its rewards.

AFTERWORD

I began writing and researching for this book over three years ago. As I watched not only my own children but also the children that I taught and administrated, I began to see trends that I discussed in earlier chapters. I truly believe that when students have enough authentic confidence to embrace challenges for their successes and failures, they achieve learning moments that are fundamental in education. This is, truly, the purpose of education. We are constantly saying that we prepare students for jobs in a world that has yet to be imagined. If we dig into that statement, are we not saying that if we give students the confidence to face new challenges that may result in trial and error, they will be able to pivot their thinking and skills naturally to adapt to new challenges? These new challenges will offer experiences that will serve adolescents with teachable moments. Youngsters can then build a reservoir of skills, which can be applied to opportunities we cannot even imagine or define today.

During the process of compiling the research for this book, I was hired to be the Head of School for Brookfield Academy in a suburb of Milwaukee. It was during my first months there, while listening and watching, that I witnessed all the individual building blocks of authentic confidence come together. I had seen them at different times in different schools in different cities, but never as a whole. The academic responsibility combined with the social responsibility of character, truth, heritage, and individuality provided opportunities for students to develop authentic confidence. It was the proof in the pudding, so to say.

I am amazed when I walk around the school and see it in action. I observe children stretching themselves academically and in other areas of life with determination and perseverance. Yes, I also see kids struggle with failure. However, I see a support mechanism in place that helps them discover how they can learn from that failure. I used some examples of this in the chapters of this book. I know there are other schools, both public and private, that I am sure can provide similar or even different ways of building authentic confidence in children. I look forward to this book providing more transparency as to what those schools are doing to build authentic confidence so that teachers can share ideas and practices.

My hope in writing this book is that we can begin a conversation about what is working in our schools to build authentic confidence. Authentic confidence shows students that through hard work, determination, and perseverance, they can set their own paths. With my own eyes, I have seen students be the firsts in their families to go to college.

I recently visited a K-8 school in inner-city Milwaukee that tracked its graduates until the end of college. This was a girls' school with a large percentage of college attendees, but only a 33% college graduation rate. They were asking great questions about this drop in numbers. Most of the students had scholarships, which left out any obvious financial arguments. So, why were they not succeeding? Could it be that we failed to develop their authentic confidence to handle the hard work and high standards of higher education? Did we adequately prepare them to face those challenges when support is not necessarily given, but has to be sought? They did not have answers, but I congratulated them on asking the questions and seeking the reasons in an attempt to advance education for female first-time college students.

Building Authentic Confidence in Children was written so that we can address a bigger issue, and stop looking for the "quick fix" or teaching to the bottom third. It offers us the opportunity to now engage all students individually, wherever they may be in their educational careers, and challenge them to grow, overcome defeat, and build a meaningful toolbox for their lives.

As I continue in the field of education, I hope to further define and outline more practical and useful tools for teachers as they aid and support students' confidence. I have been very fortunate in my life to have had experiences that offered opportunities for building my own authentic confidence. It was difficult yet beneficial, and I only wish I'd had more of those opportunities when I was in school.

We must rethink how we train our teachers and how curriculum impacts our students. We have a history of trying to quickly fix the "education problem" in the United States, rather than looking at different long-term strategies that provide results. We fail to hold our students, teachers, and parents accountable in working together to foster the confidence needed for the challenges of tomorrow. I know we can do it because I have seen it in action. Schools can and should be a learning environment, rich with experiences that challenge the perseverance and grit of a child in an effort to build his or her authentic confidence to face the trials of life. It's time to keep the conversation going and offer the gift of building authentic confidence.

REFERENCES

"The Trophy Kids Grow Up: How the Millennial Generation Is Shaking Up the Workplace." Publishers Weekly 255.32 (2008): 38. Academic Search Premier. Web. 27 Feb. 2016.

Ablow, Dr. Keith. "We Are Raising a Generation of Deluded Narcissists | Fox News." *Fox News*. FOX News Network, 08 Jan. 2013. Web. 05 June 2016.

Abrams, L. M., Pedulla, J. J., & Madaus, G. F. (2003). Views from the classroom: Teachers' opinions of statewide testing programs. Theory into Practice, 42, 18 – 29. doi: 10.1207/s15430421tip4201_4

Ainley, M. D. 1993. "Styles of Engagement with Learning: Multidimensional Assessment of their Relationship with Strategy Use and School Achievement." Journal of Educational Psychology 85 (3): 395–405. doi:10.1037/0022-0663.85.3.395.

Alsop, R. (2008, October 21). The "trophy kids" go to work. Wall Street Journal, pp.D1.

Altshuler, Sandra J., and Tresa Schmautz. "No Hispanic Student Left Behind: The Consequences of "High Stakes" Testing." Children & Schools 28.1 (2006): 5-14. Academic Search Premier. Web. 2 Mar. 2016.

Anderman, E. M., M. L. Maehr, and C. Midgley. 1999. "Declining Motivation after the Transition to Middle School: Schools can Make a Difference." Journal of Research and Development in Education 32 (3): 131–147.

Bailey, Richard. "Do Sports and Other Physical Activities Build Self-Esteem?" Psychology Today. N.p., 7 Aug. 2014. Web. 12 May 2016.

Bandura, A. 1994. "Self-efficacy." In Encyclopedia of Human Behavior, edited by V. S. Ramachaudran, 71–81. New York: Academic Press.

Bandura, A. 1997. Self-efficacy: The Exercise of Control. New York: W.H. Freeman.

Bandura, A. 2006. "Guide for Creating Self-efficacy Scales." In Self-efficacy Beliefs of Adolescent, edited by F. Pajares and T. Urdan, 307–338. Greenwich: Information Age.

Baumeister, Roy F., Jennifer D. Campbell, Joachim I. Krueger, and Kathleen D. Vohs. "Does High Self-esteem Cause Better Performance, Interpersonal Success, Happiness, or Healthier Lifestyles?" Psychological Science in the Public Interest (Wiley-Blackwell) 4.1 (2003): 1-44. Academic Search Premier. Web. 21 Feb. 2016.

Beesley, A., & Apthorp, H. (Eds.). (2010). Classroom instruction that works, second edition: Research report. Denver, CO: McRel.

Bandura, A. 1986. Social Foundations of Thought and Action: A Social Cognitive Theory. Englewood Cliffs, N.J.: Prentice-Hall.

Beyers, W. & Goossens, L. (2002). Concurrent and predictive validity of the student adaptation to college questionnaire in a sample of European freshman students. Educational and Psychological Measurement, 62, 527–538.

Beyer S. and Bowden E. (1997), "Gender Differences in Self-Perceptions: Convergent Evidence from Three Measures of Accuracy and Bias," Personality and Social Psychology Bulletin, Vol. 23, pp. 157-172.

Blatchford, P., Moriarty, V., Edmonds, S. & Martin, C. (2002) Relationships between class size and teaching: a multi-method analysis of English infant schools, American Educational Research Journal, 39(1), 101– 132.

Bong, M., and E. Skaalvik. 2003. "Academic Self-concept and Self-efficacy: How Different Are They Really?" Educational Psychology Review 15 (1): 1–40. doi: 10.1023/A:1021302408382.

Bong, M. 2006. "Asking the Right Question: How Confident Are You that You Could Successfully Perform these Tasks?" In Self-efficacy Beliefs of Adolescent, edited by F. Pajares and T. Urdan, 287–306. Greenwich: Information Age.

Bowles, T. (1999). Focusing on time orientation to explain adolescent self-concept and academic achievement: Part II. Testing a model. Journal of Applied Health Behaviour, 1, 1-8.

Branden, N. (1984, August-September). In defense of self. Association for Humanistic Psychology Newsletter, 12-13.

Brown, R., M. Pressley, P. Van Meter, and T. Schuder. 1996. "A Quasi-experimental Validation of Transactional Strategies Instruction with Low Achieving Second-grade Readers." Journal of Educational Psychology 88 (1): 18–37. doi: 10.1037/0022-0663.88.1.18.

Bunker, L.K. "The Role Play and Motor Skill Development in Building Children's Self-confidence and Self-esteem." Elementary School Journal 91.5 (1991): 467. Academic Search Premier. Web. 8 Feb. 2016. Accession Number: 9108260753; Bunker, L.K.; Source Info: May 1, Vol. 91 Issue 5, p.467.

Buote, V. M., Pancer, S. M., Pratt, M. W., Adams, G., Birnie-Lefcovitch, S., Polivy, J. & Wintre, M. G. (2007). The importance of friends: Friendship and adjustment among first-year university students Journal of Adolescent Research, 22, 665–689.

Buriel, R., Perez.W, DeMent.T, Chavez,V, & Moran,V. (1998). The relationshipof language brokering to academic performance, biculturalism, and self- efficacy among Hispanic adolescents. Hispanic Journal of Behavioral Sciences, 20, 283-29.

Burns, T. and Sinfield, S. (2003) Essential Study Skills: The complete guide to success university. London: Sage: Sage.

Bushman, B.J., & Baumeister, R.F. (1998). Threatened egotism, narcissism, self-esteem, and direct and displaced aggression: Does self-love or self-hate lead to violence? Journal of Personality and Social Psychology, 75, 219–229.

Canevello, Amy, and Jennifer Crocker. "Interpersonal Goals, Others' Regard for the Self, and Self-esteem: The Paradoxical Consequences of Self-image and Compassionate Goals." European Journal of Social Psychology Eur. J. Soc. Psychol. 41.4 (2011): 422-34. Web. 1 May 2016.

Castrovince, Anthony. "Carlos Correa Early Success Runs in Family." Major League Baseball. N.p., 08 July 2015. Web. 01 May 2016.

Charles Thompson and Jane Brodie Gregory, (2016) "Managing Millennials: A Framework for Improving Attraction, Motivation, and Retention," The Psychologist-Manager Journal, Vol. 15, Issue 4, p. 238. 12 38. Ibid, p. 240.

Chen, Grace. "10 Major Challenges Facing Public Schools." PublicSchoolReview.com. N.p., 3 Mar. 2015. Web. 05 June 2016.

Cocks, A. J. 2006. "The Ethical Maze: Finding an Inclusive Path towards Gaining Children's Agreement to Research Participation." Childhood 13 (2): 247–266. doi: 10.1177/ 0907568206062942.

Craven, R. G., Marsh, H. W., & Burnett, P. C. (2003). Cracking the self-concept enhancement conundrum: A call and blueprint for the next generation of self-concept enhancement research. In H. W. Marsh, R. G. Craven, & D. M. McInerney (Eds.), International advances in self-research (Vol. 1, pp. 91-126). Greenwich, CT: Information Age.

Dawes, L., and C. Sams. 2004. Talk Box: Speaking and Listening Activities at Key Stage 1. London: David Fulton.

Deal, J. J., Altman, D. G., & Rogelberg, S. G. (2010). Millennials at work: What we know and what we need to do (if anything). Journal of Business and Psychology, 25, 191–199.

Deaux, K. and Ennsuiller, T. (1994), "Explanations of Successful Performance on Sex Linked Traits: What is Skill for the Male is Luck for the Female," Journal of Personality and Social Psychology, Vol. 29, pp. 80-85.

Derry, S. J., R. D. Pea, B. Barron, R. A. Engle, F. Erickson, R. Goldman, B. L. Sherin, et al. 2010. "Conducting Video Research in the Learning Sciences: Guidance on Selection, Analysis, Technology and Ethics." Journal of the Learning Sciences 19 (1): 3–53. doi: 10.1080/10508400903452884.

Dickha User, O., Reuter, M. & Hilling, C. (2005). Coursework selection: A frame of reference approach using structural equation modeling. British Journal of Educational Psychology, 75, 673–688.

Doman, Kevin. "Grit: The True Story of Steve Young." DeseretNews.com. N.p., 05 Apr. 2014. Web. 01 May 2016.

Durik, A. M., Vida, M. & Eccles, J. S. (2006). Task values and ability beliefs as predictors of high school literacy choices: A developmental analysis. Journal of Educational Psychology, 98, 382–393.

Dweck, C. 1986. "Motivation Processes Affecting Learning." American Psychologist 41 (10): 1040–1048. doi:10.1037/0003-066X.41.10.1040.

Ericsson, K. A., and H. A. Simon. 1993. Protocol Analysis: Verbal Reports as Data. Revised ed. Cambridge: Bradford Books/MIT Press.

E. Määttä and S. Järvelä Tirosh, D., P. Tsamir, E. Levenson, M. Tabach, and R. Barkai. 2012. "Exploring Young Children's Self-efficacy Beliefs Related to Mathematical and Nonmathematical Tasks Performed in Kindergarten: Abused and Neglected Children and their Peers." Educational Studies in Mathematics 83 (2): 309–322. doi: 10.1007/s10649-012-9458-y.

Festinger, L. 1942, A theoretical interpretation of shifts in levels of aspiration. Psychological Review 49:235-250. 1954. A theory of social comparison processes. Human Relations 1:417-419.

Flannery, Mary. "8 Challenges for the New School Year." *Rss*, National Education Association, n.d. Web. 05 June 2016.

Fredriksson, P., Öckert, B., & Oosterbeek, H. (2013). Long-term effects of class size. The Quarterly Journal of Economics, 128(1), 249-285.

Groth, Anne. "Why Teachers Leave". Baltomire Sun. web address http://www.baltimoresun.com/news/opinion/oped/bs-ed-teacher-burnout-20151130-story.html

Galton, M., Hargreaves, L., Comber, C. & Wall, D., with Pell, A. (1999) Inside the primary classroom 20 years on (London, Routledge).

George, T.R., D.L. Feltz, and M.A. Chase. 1992. Effects of model similarity on self-efficacy and muscular endurance. Journal of Sport and Exercise Psychology 14:237-248.

George, T. R., D. L. Feltz, and M. A. Chase. 1992. "The Effects of Model Similarity on Self- efficacy and Muscular Endurance: A Second Look." Journal of Sport and Exercise Psychology 14 (3): 237–248.

Gould, D., and M. Weiss. 1981. Effect of model similarity and model self-talk on self-efficacy in muscular endurance. Journal of Sport Psychology 3:17-29.

Groth, Ann. "Why Teachers Leave." Baltimoresun.com. N.p., 30 Nov. 2015. Web. 01 May 2016.

Collins, James C. Good to Great: Why Some Companies Make the Leap--and Others Don't. New York, NY: HarperBusiness, 2001. Print.

Grau, V., and D. Whitebread. 2012. "Self and Social Regulation of Learning during Collaborative Activities in the Classroom: The Interplay of Individual and Group Cognition." Learning and Instruction 22 (6): 401–412. doi:10.1016/j.learninstruc.2012.03.003.

Hattie, J. (2008) Visible learning: A synthesis of over 800 meta-analyses relating to achievement. New York: Routledge.

Hamre, B. K., & Pianta, R. C. (2005). Can instructional and emotional support in the first-grade classroom make a difference for children at risk of school failure? Child Development, 76(5) 949–967.

Hayter, Nick, and Laura Heathcock. "Facing the Future with Confidence." Occupational Health 63.12 (2011): 24-25. Academic Search Premier. Web. 28 Feb. 2016.

Heath, S., V. Charles, G. Crow, and R. Wiles. 2007. "Informed Consent, Gatekeepers and Go-betweens: Negotiating Consent in Child- and Youth-orientated Institutions." British Educational Research Journal 33 (3): 403–417. doi: 10.1080/01411920701243651.

Hershatter, A., & Epstein, M. (2010). Millennials and the world of work: An organization and management perspective. Journal of Business & Psychology, 25, 211-223.

"Hershey Community Archives | Hershey, Milton Snavely; 1857-1945. "Hershey Community Archives | Hershey, Milton Snavely; 1857-1945. N.p., n.d. Web. 01 May 2016.

Hidi, S., and M. Ainley. 2008. "Interest and Self-regulation: Relationships between Two Variables that Influence Learning." In Motivation and Self-regulated Learning: Theory, Research and Application, edited by D. H. Schunk and B. J. Zimmerman, 78–109. Mahwah: Erlbaum.

Hidden curriculum (2014, August 26). In S. Abbott (Ed.), The glossary of education reform. Retrieved from http://edglossary.org/hidden-curriculum

Hosteler, Frederick. *The Tennessee Study of Class Size in the Early School Grades* (2008): n. page. *The Tennessee Study of Class Size in the Early School Grades.* 2 May 2008. Web. 5 Mar. 2016.

House, D. (1996). College persistence and grade outcomes: Noncognitive variables as predictors of African American, Asian American, Hispanic, Native American, and white students (Report No. HE 029-310). East Lansing, MI: National Center for Research on Teaching Learning. (Eric Document Reproduction Service No. ED397710)

Howe, N., & Strauss, W. (2003). Millennials go to college. Washington, DC: American Association of Collegiate Registrars and Admissions Officers.

Howe, Neil, Struass, William (2003). Millennial got to College. *Characteristics of the Millennial Generation.* Retrieved from https://students.rice.edu/images/students/AADV/Oweek2008 AADVResources/Characteristics%20of%20the%20Millenial%20Generation.pdf

Kay, Katty, and Claire Shipman. The Confidence Code: The Science and Art of Self-assurance--what Women Should Know. N.p.: n.p., n.d. Print.

"Lack of Confidence Is Holding Back Womens' Careers." The Guardian. Guardian News and Media, 14 Aug. 2013. Web. 29 Feb. 2016.

"Center for Women's Global Leadership." SpringerReference (n.d.): n. pag. KPMG. 2015. Web. 29 Feb. 2016.

Kleitman, Sabina. Metacognition in the Rationality Debate: Self-confidence and Its Calibration. Saarbücken, Germany: VDM VerlagDr. Müller, 2008. Print.

"KPMG Women's Leadership." KPMG Women's Leadership. N.p., 2015.Web. 01 May 2016.

Kraus, Nina, Joan Hornickel, Dana Strait, Jessica Slater, and Elaine Thompson. "Engagement in Community Music Classes Sparks Neuroplasticity and Language Development in Children from Disadvantaged Backgrounds." Frontiers. N.p., 14 Dec. 2014. Web. 01 May 2016.

Krulak, Charles C. "The Fourteen Basic Traits of Effective Leadership." About Campus 3.4 (1998): 8. Academic Search Premier. Web. 8 Feb. 2016.

L, Stankov, and Kleitman S. "Process on the Borderline between Cognitive Ability and Personality: Confidence and Realism." The SAGE Handbook of Personality Theory and Assessment. Los Angeles, CA: SAGE Publications, 2008. 541-55. Print.

Leo, John. "We're All Number 1." U.S. News & World Report 124.24 (1998): 23. Academic Search Premier. Web. 28 Feb. 2016.

Liew, J., E. McTigue, L. Barrois, and J. Hughes. 2008. "Adaptive and Effortful Control and Academic Self-efficacy Beliefs on Achievement: A Longitudinal Study of 1st through 3rd Graders." Early Childhood Research Quarterly 23 (4): 515–526. doi: 10.1016/j.ecresq.2008. 07.003. International Journal of Early Years Education 323.

Littleton, K., N. Mercer, L. Dawes, R. Wegerif, D. Rowe, and C. Sams. 2005. "Talking and Thinking Together at Key Stage 1." Early Years 25 (2): 167–182. doi: 10.1080/ 09575140500128129.

A taxonomy for learning, teaching, and assessing: a revision of Bloom's taxonomy of educational objectives, New York: Longman, c2001.

Lowery, J.W. (2004). Student affairs for a new generation. New Direction for Student Services, 106, 87-98.

Maclellan, Effie. "How Might Teachers Enable Learner Self-confidence? A Review Study." Educational Review 66.1 (2014): 59-74. PsycINFO. Web. 8 Feb. 2016.

Maddux, J. E. 2002. "Self-efficacy: The Power of Believing You Can." In Handbook of Positive Psychology, edited by C. R. Snyder and S. J. Lopez, 277–287. New York: Oxford University Press.

Marsh, H.W. (1990).The structure of academic self- concept: The Marsh-Shavelson Model.Jouraa/ of Educational Psychology, 82, 623-636.

Mcinerney, Dennis M., Rebecca Wing-yi Cheng, Magdalena Mo Ching Mok, and Amy Kwok Hap Lam. "Academic Self-Concept and Learning Strategies: Direction of Effect on Student Academic Achievement." Journal of Advanced Academics 23.3 (2012): 249-69. Academic Search Premier. Web. 3 Mar. 2016.

Marsh, H. W., Craven, R. G., & McInerney, D. M. (2005). Introduction. In H. W. Marsh, R. G. Craven, & D. M. McInerney (Eds.), International advances in self-research (Vol. 2, pp. 3-13). Greenwich, CT: Information Age.

Martin, Jay. The Best of Soccer Journal, the Art of Coaching. Maidenhead: Meyer & Meyer Sport, 2015. Print.

McVeigh, Tracy. "Can Women Really Restart Their Career after Quitting Work for Children?" The Guardian. Guardian News and Media, 15 June 2013. Web. 01 May 2016.

Meister, Jeanne, and Karie Willyerd. "Mentoring Millennials." Harvard Business Review. N.p., 01 May 2010. Web. 01 May 2016.

Mentoring Millennials, Jeanne C. Meister & Karie Willyerd, FROM THE MAY HBR 2010 ISSUE.

Millennials Go To College (2003) by Neil Howe and William Strauss. Website: www.lifecourse.com.

Mooney, S. P., Sherman, M. F. & Lopresto, C. T. (1991). Academic locus of control, self-esteem, and perceived distance from home as predictors of college adjustment. Journal of Counseling and Development, 69, 445–448.

Multon, K. D., S. D. Brown, and R. W. Lent. 1991. "Relation of Self-efficacy Beliefs to Academic Outcomes: A Meta-analytic Investigation." Journal of Counseling Psychology 38 (1): 30–38. doi:10.1037/0022-0167.38.1.30.

Määttä, E., H. Järvenoja, and S. Järvelä. 2012. "Triggers of Students' Efficacious Interaction in Collaborative Learning Situations." Small Group Research 43 (4): 497–522. doi: 10.1177/ 1046496412437208.

Määttä, Elina, and Sanna Järvelä. "Involving Children in Reflective Discussions about Their Perceived Self-efficacy and Learning Experiences." International Journal of Early Years Education 21.4 (2013): 309-24. Academic Search Premier. Web. 22 Feb. 2016.

Napoli, A. R. & Wortman, P. M. (1998). Psychosocial factors related to retention and early departure of two-year community college students. Research in Higher Education, 39, 419–455.

Nolen, S. B. 2007. "The Development of Motivation to Read and Write in Young Children: Development in Social Contexts." Cognition and Instruction 25 (2–3): 219–270. doi: 10.1080/ 07370000701301174.

O'Brian, Sarah. "How I Got into 8 Ivy Leagues and 13 Other Schools." CNNMoney. Cable News Network, 7 Apr. 2016. Web. 01 May 2016.

Pajares, F., and M. D. Miller. 1994. "Role of Self-efficacy and Self-concept Beliefs in Mathematical Problem Solving: A Path Analysis." Journal of Educational Psychology 86 (2): 193–203. doi:10.1037/0022-0663.86.2.193.

Pajares, F., M. D. Miller, and M. J. Johnson. 1999. "Gender Differences in Writing Self-beliefs of Elementary School Students." Journal of Educational Psychology 91 (1): 50–61. doi: 10.1037/ 0022-0663.91.1.50.

Pajares, F. 1996. "Self-efficacy Beliefs in Academic Settings." Review of Educational Research 66 (4): 543–578. doi: 10.3102/00346543066004543.

Pajares, F. 2003. "Self-efficacy Beliefs, Motivation and Achievement in Writing: A Review of the Literature." Reading Writing Quarterly 19 (2): 139–158. doi: 10.1080/10573560308222.

Pajares, F. 2006. Self-efficacy during Childhood and Adolescence." In Self-efficacy Beliefs of Adolescent, edited by F. Pajares and T. Urdan, 307–338. Greenwich: Information Age.

Palmer, D. H. 2006. "Sources of Self-efficacy in a Science Methods Course for Primary Teacher Education Students." Research in Science Education 36 (4): 337–353. doi: 10.1007/s11165-005- 9007-0.

Patrick, H., A. M. Ryan, and A. Kaplan. 2007. "Early Adolescents' Perceptions of the Classroom Social Environment, Motivational Beliefs and Engagement." Journal of Educational Psycho- logy 99 (1): 83–98. doi: 10.1037/0022-0663.99.1.83.

Paulsen, Alisa M., and Nancy E. Betz. "Basic Confidence Predictors of Career Decision-Making Self-Efficacy." Career Development Quarterly 52.4 (2004): 354-62. Business Source Premier. Web. 8 Feb. 2016.

Perry, N. E., and K. J. O. VandeKamp. 2000. "Creating Classroom Contexts that Support Young Children's Development of Self-regulated Learning." International Journal of Educational Research 33 (7–8): 821–843. doi: 10.1016/S0883-0355(00)00052-5.

Perry, N. E., L. Phillips, and L. R. Hutchinson. 2006. "Mentoring Student Teachers to Support Self-regulated Learning." The Elementary School Journal 106 (3): 237–254. doi: 10.1086/501485.

Perry, N. E. 1998. "Young Children's Self-regulated Learning and Contexts that Support It." Journal of Educational Psychology 90: 715–729. doi: 10.1037/0022-0663.90.4.715.

Pintrich, P. 2004. "A Conceptual Framework for Assessing Motivation and Self-regulated Learning in College Students." Educational Psychology Review 16 (4): 385–407. doi: 10.1007/s10648- 004-0006-x.

REINDERS, MARY. "MYSO – Instrumental in Changing Lives." MYSO. N.p., Dec. 2015. Web. 30 Apr. 2016.

Rönnau-Böse, M., & Fröhlich-Gildhoff, K. (2009). The Promotion of Resilience: A Person-Centered Perspective of Prevention in Early Childhood Institutions. Person-Centered & Experiential Psychotherapies, 8(4), 299-318.

Rutherford, Markella. "The Social Value of Self-Esteem." Society 48.5 (2011): 407-12. Academic Search Premier. Web. 21 Feb. 2016.

Ryan, A. M. 2001. "The Peer Group as a Context for the Development of Young Adolescent Motivation and Achievement." Child Development 72 (4): 1135–1150. doi: 10.1111/1467- 8624.00338.

Saarni, C., J. J. Campos, L. Camras, and D. Witherington. 2006. "Emotional Development: Action, Communication and Understanding." In Handbook of Child Psychology, edited by W. Damon and N. Eisenberg, 237–254. New York: John Wiley.

Samuels, Mina. Run like a Girl: How Strong Women Make Happy Lives. Berkeley, CA: Seal, 2011. Print.

Schanzenbach, Diane Whitmore, "Does Class Size Matter?" National Education Policy Center. N.p., n.d. February 2014. Web. 06 Mar. 2016.

Schunk, D. H., and J. L. Meece. 2006. "Self-efficacy Development in Adolescence." In Self-efficacy Beliefs of Adolescent, edited by F. Pajares and T. Urdan, 71–96. Greenwich: Information Age. Seifert, T. 2004. "Understanding Student Motivation." Educational Research 46 (2): 137–149. doi: 10.1080/0013188042000222421.

Schunk, D. H. 1991. "Self-efficacy and Academic Motivation." Educational Psychologist 26 (3): 207–231. doi: 10.1207/s15326985ep2603&4_2.

Segool, Natasha K., John S. Carlson, Anisa N. Goforth, Nathan Von Der Embse, and Justin A. Barterian. "Heightened Test Anxiety among Young Children: Elementary School Students' Anxious Responses to High-stakes Testing." Psychology in the Schools 50.5 (2013): 489-99. Academic Search Premier. Web. 6 Mar. 2016.

"Self Confidence Tips for College Students." Stanford University. N.p., n.d. Web. 12 May 2016.

Shapiro, Rees. "Fairfax Schools Chief Calls for $96 Million in Budget Cuts." *Washington Post*. The Washington Post, 9 Jan. 2014. Web. 05 June 2016.

Skaalvik, E.M., and Hagtvet, K.A. (1990). Academic Achievement and self-concept, and conformity to school norms: A developmental analysis. Zeitschrift Fur Paragogische Psycholgie, 9, 211-220.

Skinner, E. A., and M. J. Belmont. 1993. "Motivation in the Classroom: Reciprocal Effects of Teacher Behavior and Student Engagement across the School Year." Journal of Educational Psychology 85 (4): 571–581. doi: 10.1037/0022-0663.85.4.571. 324

Shipman, Claire, and Katty Kay. "The Confidence Gap." The Atlantic. Atlantic Media Company, May 2014. Web. 01 May 2016.

Steinmetz, Katy, and Josh Sanburn. "Move Over, Millennials." Time 186.27/28 (2015): 134. Academic Search Premier. Web. 27 Feb. 2016.

"The Condition of Education 2014." The Condition of Education 2014. N.p., May 2014. Web. 01 May 2016.

"Top Eight Challenges Teachers Face This School Year - NEA Today." NEA Today. N.p., 13 Sept. 2010. Web. 12 May 2016.

Thompson, Charles, and Jane Brodie Gregory. "Managing Millennials: A Framework for Improving Attraction, Motivation, and Retention." The Psychologist-Manager Journal 15.4 (2012): 237-46. PsycARTICLES. Web. 28 Feb. 2016.

Toth, Joan. "Closing the Confidence Gap." Convenience Store News 52.1 (2016): 90-91. Business Source Premier. Web. 29 Feb. 2016.

Triplett, C. F., & Barksdale, M. A. (2005). Third through sixth graders' perceptions of high-stakes testing. Journal of Literacy Research, 37, 237 – 260. Retrieved from http://www.nrconline.org/cgi/jlrlibrary.cgi.

Tulley, Gever. *Beware Dangerism*. TED Books, 2011. Digital Print.

Twenge, Jean M., and W. Keith. Campbell. The Narcissism Epidemic: Living in the Age of Entitlement. New York: Free, 2009. Print.

Usher, E. L., and F. Pajares. 2009. "Sources of Self-efficacy in Mathematics: A Validation Study." Contemporary Educational Psychology 34 (1): 89–101. doi: 10.1016/j.cedpsych.2008.09.002.

Usher, E. L. 2008. "Sources of Middle School Students' Self-efficacy in Mathematics: A Qualitative Investigation of Student, Teacher and Parent Perspectives." American Educational Research Journal 46 (1): 275–314. doi: 10.3102/0002831208324517.

Van Dinther, M., F. Dochy, and M. Segers. 2011. "Factors Affecting Students' Self-efficacy in Higher Education." Educational Research Review 6 (2): 95–108. doi: 10.1016/j.edurev.2010. 10.003.

Weissmann, Jordan. "America's Awful College Dropout Rates, in Four Charts." Slate Magazine. N.p., 19 Nov. 2014. Web. 01 May 2016.

Wentzel, K. R. 1999. "Social-motivational Processes and Interpersonal Relationships: Implications for Understanding Students' Academic Success." Journal of Educational Psychology 91: 76–97. doi: 10.1037/0022-0663.91.1.76.

Whitebread, D., and P. Coltman. 2007. "Developing Young Children as Self-regulating Learners." In Beginning Teaching: Beginning Learning in Primary Education, edited by J. Moyles, 154–168. London: Open University Press/McGraw Hill Education.

Wilson, K. M., and G. Trainin. 2007. "First Grade Students' Motivation and Achievement for Reading, Writing and Spelling." Reading Psychology 28 (3): 257–282. doi: 10.1080/ 02702710601186464.

Whitebread, D. 2012. Developmental Psychology and Early Childhood Education. A Guide for Students and Practitioners. Thousand Oaks, CA: SAGE.

Whitebread, D., S. Bingham, V. Grau, D. P. Pasternak, and C. Sangster. 2007. "Development of Metacognition and Self-regulated Learning in Young Children: Role of Collaborative and Peer- assisted Learning." Journal of Cognitive Education and Psychology 6 (3): 433–455. doi:10.1891/194589507787382043.

Wiggins, Grant P., and Jay McTighe. Understanding by Design. Alexandria, VA: Association for Supervision and Curriculum Development, 1998. Print.

Williams, J. D. (2003). Student engagement at school: A sense of belonging and participation. Paris, France: OECD.

Winne, P. H., and N. E. Perry. 2000. "Measuring Self-regulated Learning." In Handbook of Self- regulation, edited by P. Pintrich, M. Boekaerts, and M. Seidner, 531–566. Orlando: Academic Press.

Wouters, Sofie, Veerle Germeijs, Hilde Colpin, and Karine Verschueren. "Academic Self-concept in High School: Predictors and Effects on Adjustment in Higher Education." Scandinavian Journal of Psychology 52.6 (2011): 586-94. Academic Search Premier. Web. 3 Mar. 2016.

Wyer, Kathy. "Grads of All-girls Schools Show Stronger Academic Orientations than Coed Grads." UCLA Newsroom. N.p., 19 Mar. 2009. Web. 01 May 2016.

Zimmerman, B. J., and A. Bandura, and M. Martinez-Pons. 1992. "Self-motivation for Academic Attainment: The Role of Self-efficacy Beliefs and Personal Goal Setting." American Educational Journal 29 (3): 663–676. doi: 10.3102/00028312029003663.

Zimmerman, B. J., and A. Bandura. 1994. "Impact of Self-regulatory Influences on Writing Course Attainment." American Educational Research Journal 31: 845–862. doi: 10.3102/00028312031004845.

Zimmerman, B. J., and A. Kitsantas. 2005. "The Hidden Dimension of Personal Competence: Self-regulated Learning and Practice." In Handbook of Competence and Motivation, edited by A. J. Elliot and C. S. Dweck, 204–222. New York: Guilford Press.

Zimmerman, B. J., and D. H. Schunk. 2008. "Motivation: An Essential Dimension of Self-regulated Learning." In Motivation and Self-regulated Learning: Theory, Research and Applications, edited by D. H. Schunk and B. J. Zimmerman, 1–30. Mahwah: Erlbaum.

Zimmerman, B. J. 2000. "Attaining Self-regulation: A Social Cognitive Perspective." In Handbook of Self-regulation, edited by M. Boekaerts, P. Pintrich, and M. Zeidner, 13–39. New York: Academic Press.

Zimmerman, B. J. 2002. "Becoming a Self-regulated Learner: An Overview." Theory into Practice 41 (2): 64–70. doi: 10.1207/s15430421tip4102_2.

Zwick, Joel. "Girl Meets World - Girl Meets STEM - Video Dailymotion." *Dailymotion.* Disney Channel, 9 Jan. 2016. Web. 05 June 2016.

ABOUT THE AUTHORS

Dr. Spencer Taintor

Dr. Taintor has dedicated his life to the betterment of education and those who experience it. A graduate of the University of Miami, Florida, and Capella University in Minneapolis, his diverse experiences in professional leadership, corporate business, and marketing offered him a unique and in-depth perspective of how learning and self-worth affects individuals on a daily basis in many different parts of the United States. In 2003, Dr. Taintor fully entered the world of the classroom as a chemistry teacher and later Dean of Students for Gulliver Schools in Pinecrest, Florida. He continued on in education as a Headmaster at several institutions before becoming Head of School at Brookfield Academy in Brookfield, Wisconsin. He resides with his wife and two children in the greater Milwaukee area.

RaeAnne Marie Scargall

A student of Naropa University and a graduate of the University of Wisconsin-Whitewater, RaeAnne carries a degree in publishing and an intensive editorial and collaborative writing background. She is a veritable Jane-of-all-writin–g-trades addition to the Reji Laberje Writing and Publishing team. Matched with Dr. Taintor due to their shared love for and expertise in writing with and for educators, RaeAnne has relished the co-writing partnership with him. RaeAnne lives with her sous chef fiancé outside of Milwaukee, Wisconsin.